SIGNS OF SEVEN THUNDERS

PREPARE *Ye A* HIGHWAY

A LATTER-DAY PERSPECTIVE *on the* SIGNS OF OUR TIMES

PRAISE FOR

Prepare Ye a Highway

As a young adult, I was naturally drawn toward Church books that combined doctrine with historical events to illustrate God's big, macro plan for His children. Names like Smith, McConkie, and Maxwell were but a few of my favorite reads. Unfortunately, these types of doctrinal-historical overviews are rare these days. Thus, it is so refreshing to find this gem by Drew Williams. You will immediately notice that this book was not slapped together in a day. It is both deep and broad. Anyone who reads it will know that Drew spent years reflecting, conceptualizing, indexing, and building layer-by-layer scriptural, political, cultural, and spiritual insights of great worth. The genius of this book, however, is not just the content—it is Drew's quick wit and command of the language. He has a way with words, and it is definitely entertaining. He does a masterful job at bringing in his wry sense of humor to illustrate the hubris of man juxtaposed to the absolute omniscience, justice, and mercy of God. This book is a top recommend for lay person or scholar, and especially anyone who thinks seriously about scriptural prophecy and its fulfillment.

—Richard J. McClendon, PhD
Noted author and coauthor of *Commitment to the Covenant*

I am usually leery of endorsing any book about future events. However, after reading Drew's manuscript, my apprehension was swept away. The reason? Because of his heavy use of scripture to reinforce his ideas. *Prepare Ye a Highway* will give each reader a wonderful, eye-opening experience and a solid foundation concerning what the Lord has said through ancient and modern prophets, as well as the teachings of numerous scholars, concerning his return and the end of days. Drew's unique writing style leaves the reader feeling like they just exited Drew's office after a pleasant chat next to a fire.

—Jack R. Christianson, PhD
Retired religious educator and best-selling author

SIGNS OF SEVEN THUNDERS

PREPARE *Ye A* HIGHWAY

A LATTER-DAY PERSPECTIVE *on the* SIGNS OF OUR TIMES

DREW BLANDFORD-WILLIAMS

CFI
AN IMPRINT OF CEDAR FORT, INC.
SPRINGVILLE, UTAH

This is not an official publication of The Church of Jesus Christ of Latter-day Saints. The opinions and views expressed herein belong solely to the author and do not necessarily represent the opinions or views of Cedar Fort, Inc. Permission for the use of sources, graphics, and photos is also solely the responsibility of the author.

ISBN 13: 978-1-4621-4315-3

Published by CFI, an imprint of Cedar Fort, Inc.
2373 W. 700 S., Springville, UT 84663
Distributed by Cedar Fort, Inc., www.cedarfort.com

Library of Congress Control Number: 2022937784

Cover design by Shawnda T. Craig

Printed in the United States of America

10 9 8 7 6 5 4 3 2 1

Printed on acid-free paper

CONTENTS

PREFACE

Eschatology*. It's a fancy word invented by Greek scholars that ascribes the fate of the human soul after mortality does away with the body. Many cultures and faiths have their own interpretation of what becomes of us in the hereafter. The Hindus have their "Kalpa" cycles.[1] For Buddhists, it's all about "Bodhi" and the enlightenment that may be earned.[2] And for the people of Scandinavia, it's Ragnarök! (No, not that one!)[3]

Conversely, Jewish eschatology contends that a final judgment for the human race is a debated topic. Some Jewish scholars insist, based on their interpretation of Talmudic law, that a resurrection of the dead, which is called *t'chiyat hameitim* in Hebrew, will take place while others argue that no judgment (or resurrection) is needed, because of Rosh Hashanah, which is an annual day of judgment.[4] Additional thoughts on the matter suggest that only those from the "Gentile nations" will be judged and not the children of Judah.

These past 5,000 years and perhaps even earlier, however, have revealed a history of the human race that has many cultures, countries, and creeds, including everything from the stars, sea, forests, and

1. https://baharna.com/karma/yuga.htm
2. https://www.newworldencyclopedia.org/entry/Bodhi
3. https://www.britannica.com/event/Ragnarok
4. https://www.myjewishlearning.com/article/jewish-resurrection-of-the-dead/

mountains in their doctrines and dogma, regarding three relevant questions:

1. Who are we?
2. Why are we here?
3. What happens next (and when)?

Now, in the midst of a flourishing pandemic, and following a twenty-year war in the very land where most of today's "Western" religious ideas (along with a few others) originated, people are returning to these ages-old questions. And whether it be the internet, online fraud, televangelists, or hostile nation-states, there are plenty of influences to sway and confuse the naive and unassuming into thinking all is lost. But such is not the case, and is the focus of this book.

The mere idea of our very existence being tested is as old a concept as is our tenure on the earth. Since the beginning of recorded time, mankind has faced challenges that have forced us to become stronger, adapt to changing circumstances, overcome obstacles, and recover to monumental levels of achievement.

Nearly four centuries before Christ walked the earth, the great Chinese sage, Confucius, wrote: "Our greatest glory is not in never failing, but in rising every time we fail.[5]"

During what historians might agree was something of a far simpler era, when many of our ancestors were not much more than nomadic tribes roaming the countryside, a prophet named Isaiah foretold of a time when the world would find itself pounding swords into plowshares. Further to Isaiah's powerful words of encouragement, and made famous by Charles Jennens when his friend, George Handel, put them to music, the ancient prophet counseled that if we make "straight in the desert a highway for our God," his glory will be revealed, and our burdens may become lightened:

> Prepare ye the way of the Lord, make straight in the desert a highway for our God. Every valley shall be exalted, and every mountain and hill shall be made low: and the crooked shall be made straight, and

---

5. https://plato.stanford.edu/entries/confucius/

> the rough places plain: and the glory of the Lord shall be revealed, and all flesh shall see it together. (Isaiah 40)

Isaiah notwithstanding, many ancient and revered oracles and prophets have warned subsequent generations to exercise caution regarding seeking for signs of the times, adding the stipulation that those who are prepared and can recognize the foreshadowing symbols, should not live in fear, but face the reality that no one escapes their mortal fate:

> Await not in quiet the coming of the horses, the marching feet, the armed host upon the land. Slip away. Turn your back. You will meet in battle anyway. (Oracle at Delphi, 480 BC)

In theory, the idea of turning our attention away from war, conquest, and self-interest implies a noble and worthy intention. However, our history reveals a different reality. For more than twenty centuries, prophets, astronomers, philosophers, and even politicians have pondered the timeline and life expectancy of the human race. During the first century, Christians referred to the "Epiphany," or epiphanaeia, to indicate the visit of the Magi upon the birth of Christ,[6] and in a broader sense, it refers to a revelatory appearance by Christ in His resurrected glory.

In his apocryphal writings recorded in the book of Revelation, the Apostle John wrote of signs and symbols that suggested not only his own liberation from his exile on Patmos but also foreshadowing of things to come, of which he was permitted to observe but not record:

> And he had in his hand a little book open: and he set his right foot upon the sea, and his left foot on the earth, and cried with a loud voice, as when a lion roareth: and when he had cried, seven thunders uttered their voices. And when the seven thunders had uttered their voices, I was about to write: and I heard a voice from heaven saying

6. https://www.christianity.com/wiki/holidays/is-epiphany-three-kings-day-a-biblical-holiday.html

> unto me, Seal up those things which the seven thunders uttered, and write them not. (Revelation 10:2–3)

When will the End of Days actually occur? Some scholars suggest the end has already begun. If current affairs in the Middle East (or even closer to home) are any indication that humanity's clock may be winding down, references by early church leaders shortly after the death of Christ suggest Christian eschatology might be more foreseeable than formerly anticipated.[7]

Christianity follows the line of thought that all souls will come to be judged after the world of the mortal man has ended and that the righteous will be united with Jesus at His coming, being spared God's angry wrath upon the world, while there will be (literally) "hell to pay" for those who have chosen wickedness as a way of life. The Born-again world calls this the "Rapture" (a somewhat adapted French/ Latin word with various references to being taken up in the clouds but lacking any relevant scriptural credibility or reference).

Now, almost 2,000 years since Jesus first began His mortal ministry, we continue to look for Him, even as we walk among the very times foreseen by Paul:

> Men shall be lovers of their own selves, covetous, boasters, proud, blasphemers, disobedient to parents, unthankful, unholy, without natural affection, trucebreakers, false accusers, incontinent, fierce, despisers of those that are good, traitors, heady, high-minded, lovers of pleasures more than lovers of God; having a form of godliness but denying the power thereof: from such turn away. (2 Timothy 3:1–5)

Many cultures throughout history have claimed to know when the Lord will return, despite the fact that the scriptures report even Christ not being aware of the actual date and time of His grand reunion with the world.[8]

---

7. https://www.history.com/topics/religion/religions-on-the-end-of-the-world
8. https://www.ldsliving.com/5-second-coming-myths-and-the-truth-behind-them/s/76618

The question may be, then, not whether there is a plan for man or whether Christ will return and when. More poignantly, the debate as to whether the human race is prepared for the inevitable coming of "the great and dreadful day of the Lord" will continue,[9] likely, right up to the point where the trumpets sound and the thunders roareth.

And while scripture does imply that the righteous will delight in the Second Coming of the Savior, while the wicked will be found cowering in the shadows, there is still much deliberation over who will be found standing in holy places during those closing moments of man, and who will stand as a witness for the judgment.[10] In Malachi 3 we read: "And I will come near to you to judgment; and I will be a swift witness against the sorcerers, and against the adulterers, and against false swearers, and against those that oppress the hireling in his wages, the widow, and the fatherless, and that turn aside the stranger from his right, and fear not me, saith the Lord of hosts."

Regardless, however, these events pertaining to the fate of the human soul may be contested by us as individuals, but they cannot be ignored. Adding to the nature of humans to follow what modern philosophers call the "pride cycle," and we begin to identify patterns throughout history that shows the human race as various segments of it passes through this book's interpretation of the pride cycle:[11]

- Captivity
- Humility
- Recovery
- Prosperity
- Arrogance
- Collapse

---

9. https://www.churchofjesuschrist.org/study/manual/old-testament-gospel-doctrine-teachers-manual/lesson-48?lang=eng&cid=14503511667&adlang=eng&source=google&network=x&gclid=Cj0KCQiAhMOMBhDhARIsAPVml-HJ48DSY4jfv4bwGDeyIfbhB-o67u6iUHIWnkqlngB3_0pPy1DZlsQaAp6nEALw_wcB&gclid=Cj0KCQiAhMOMBhDhARIsAPVml-HJ48DSY4jfv4bwGDeyIfbhB-o67u6iUHIWnkqlngB3_0pPy1DZlsQaAp6nEALw_wcB
10. https://www.thechurchnews.com/archives/2000-04-01/what-does-it-mean-to-stand-as-witness-119825
11. https://stephenblandino.com/2015/08/the-four-stages-in-the-cycle-of-pride.html

This book is an attempt to capture several thousand years' worth of signs and present them in a fashion that might help us—not in any way that places doubt on the events that have transpired, or on those that are foreseen, but rather, how we as a people may prepare ourselves for what may or may not occur in our lifetime.

Part I
They Shall Be Led Captive

"All we have yet heard, and we have experienced is scarcely a preface to the sermon that is going to be preached. When the testimony of the Elders ceases to be given, and the Lord says to them, "Come home; I will now preach my own sermons to the nations of the earth," all you now know can scarcely be called a preface to the sermon that will be preached with fire and sword, tempests, earthquakes, hail, rain, thunders and lightnings, and fearful destruction. What matters the destruction of a few railway cars? You will hear of magnificent cities, now idolized by the people, sinking in the earth, entombing the inhabitants. The sea will heave itself beyond its bounds, engulfing mighty cities. Famine will spread over the nations and nation will rise up against nation, kingdom against kingdom and states against states, in our own country and in foreign lands; and they will destroy each other, caring not for the blood and lives of their neighbors, of their families, or for their own lives."

—Brigham Young, 1860[1]

1. https://journalofdiscourses.com/Brigham_Young

And so, we begin. It's amazing how something spoken just over 160 years ago has already come to pass time and again. When Brigham Young gave his prophetic speech to a relatively new population of pioneer immigrants to the Salt Lake Valley, the United States was still three years away from the Civil War, and the world had not seen such immense destruction as would follow in the coming decades of the twentieth century.

There are many publications that outline perspectives on the last days. In fact, much of this work is a revision of an earlier book, *33 Ways God is Preparing the World for the Second Coming*, but with an expanded perspective on matters of faith and signs that all is not hopeless.

As we have seen in recent years, for Christians everywhere, there is no reason to hide from the realities that signs relating to climate change, warring nations, a pandemic, and wholesale corruption have become standard fare for the human race to consider as "the coming of the end of days." And while we are often burdened with 24/7 news of impending doom, conflicts that abound and new reasons to never go out in public being posted in social media at every turn, the one constant that humans seem to do really well is live with the hope that things will get better.

And no better example of what some might refer to as "hopeless optimism" has been displayed throughout history during those times when whole nations have been made to serve a dominating force, and still overcome the odds to become successful, thriving cultures.

Robert F. Kennedy said, "Each time a man stands up for an ideal, or acts to improve the lot of others, or strikes out against injustice, he sends forth a tiny ripple of hope."[2]

For as long as humans have roamed the earth, there have been those who have had a desire to dominate everyone else. In times of war, taking prisoners or "capturing" an enemy (or an entire race as in Word War II), was a common occurrence. For the unfortunate among the ranks of the conquered, the men were made to be slaves, and the women and children were sold for nefarious purposes.

2. https://www.brainyquote.com/quotes/robert_kennedy_745908

Our study begins in ancient times, during a period when the ancient tribes of Israel were taken, enslaved, or assimilated (being forced to blend their DNA into the bloodlines of their captive hosts), by those people commonly referred to as the "Gentile Nations."

> Then let them which are in Judaea flee to the mountains; and let them which are in the midst of it depart out; and let not them that are in the countries enter thereinto. Or these be the days of vengeance, that all things which are written may be fulfilled. But woe unto them that are with child, and to them that give suck, in those days! for there shall be great distress in the land, and wrath upon this people. And they shall fall by the edge of the sword and shall be led away captive into all nations: and Jerusalem shall be trodden down of the Gentiles. (Luke 21)

But who are these "Gentiles" and how did they come to get such bad press throughout history?

As the prophets of the Bible chronicle their plight through history, those tribes referred to as "Gentiles" include any group who are not considered the children of Israel, and their "time" refers to the period when these Gentiles will reign as world powers, which include domination of the children of Israel—something that continued into the early twentieth century.

After Jerusalem fell to King Nebuchadnezzar II of Babylon in 597 BC, the people of Judah began more than 2,000 years of history that has been peppered with being subject to captivity by stronger nations and as the nation of Israel was almost cast into oblivion.

Poor Jerusalem. As history has recorded, it would seem that everyone has taken a shot at its people, politics, religion, and most precious son: a man called "Yeshua ben Youssef" (Jesus of Nazareth).

Like grafted branches into a fruit tree, the original chosen people of God, many scholars suggest, must be grafted into the kingdom of God by recognizing the atonement and redemption by the very man who they purchased for execution more than 2,000 years ago.

In the ancient times before their fall, prophets from both kingdoms—Israel in the north and Judah in the south—foresaw a time when the age of man would be dominated by Gentiles, but in the last days, following great success, strife, conquest, and calamity, a Son of David would return and take his place as Ruler of Nations:

> I will gather all nations against Jerusalem to battle; and the city shall be taken, and the houses rifled, and the women ravished; and half of the city shall go forth into captivity, and the residue of the people shall not be cut off from the city. Then shall the Lord go forth, and fight against those nations, as when he fought in the day of battle. And his feet shall stand in that day upon the mount of Olives, which is before Jerusalem on the east, and the mount of Olives shall cleave in the midst thereof toward the east and toward the west, and there shall be a very great valley; and half of the mountain shall remove toward the north, and half of it toward the south. (Zechariah 14)

Modern analysis of biblical references to the times of the Gentiles may suggest that this passage refers to the Lord administering His retribution onto a wicked world, as further referenced by traditional Old Testament and Talmudic doctrine. In the traditional Hebrew writings found throughout the Old Testament, "those who are in Judea flee[ing] to the mountains" refers not to the retribution of any particular nation or people, but more likely refers to God's final judgment against those who would stand against Him.[3]

Fast forward five centuries, and once again we see a continued history of affliction and captivity. But why? Why were the children of Israel so selected?

After reflecting on what would become the destruction of Jerusalem because of their pride and continued disobedience to God's desires for them—both as a nation and as a people—Jesus referred to a time in which Gentile nations would reign over His people "until the appointed time of nations." In the epistle of Luke, Jesus refers to a period when "the times of the Gentiles are fulfilled."

---

3. https://creationconcept.wordpress.com/2012/07/03/flee-to-which-mountains/

> They will fall by the edge of the sword and be led captive among all nations, and Jerusalem will be trampled underfoot by the Gentiles, until the times of the Gentiles are fulfilled. (Luke 21)

Many perspectives abound on what and when the "times of the Gentiles"[4] may be or have been. The virtual annihilation of the Christian population by Nero in AD 70 and the fall and pillaging of Jerusalem in 71 by Vespasian and his brother, Titus Andronicus, might be considered valid examples in ancient history in which the "Gentiles" of Rome were doing some heavy trampling.

At the bottom of Palatine Hill, in what is now the remnant of ancient Rome, the Arch of Titus still stands and depicts visual references to the fall of Jerusalem and the temple of the Jews. In what many scholars suggest yet another sign of Jesus's words fulfilled, the Jewish revolts against their Roman occupiers throughout the first century, led to the total destruction of their temple:

> The rebels shortly after attacked the Romans again, and a clash followed between the guards of the sanctuary and the troops who were putting out the fire inside the inner court; the latter routed the Jews and followed in hot pursuit right up to the Temple itself. Then one of the soldiers, without awaiting any orders and with no dread of so momentous a deed, but urged on by some supernatural force, snatched a blazing piece of wood and, climbing on another soldier's back, hurled the flaming brand through a low golden window that gave access, on the north side, to the rooms that surrounded the sanctuary. As the flames shot up, the Jews let out a shout of dismay that matched the tragedy; they flocked to the rescue, with no thought of sparing their lives or husbanding their strength; for the sacred structure that they had constantly guarded with such devotion was vanishing before their very eyes. (Josephus Flavius [AD 70])[5]

---

4. http://eom.byu.edu/index.php/Gentiles,_Fulness_of
5. http://www.eyewitnesstohistory.com/jewishtemple.htm

With their sacred city occupied, their temple in flames, and their people butchered, the flames continued to burn in the old city while soldiers pillaged and Caesar toured the town. Tracts of land were reapportioned to Roman leaders, and Jewish families were disbursed and eventually absorbed into the Roman tapestry.

But beyond the logistics of one tribe conquering another, scholars and historians have debated the meaning of the "times of the Gentiles," although many agree that the period of uprising against the children of Israel has more to do with the rise of nations not associated with Judaism but those that developed based on the other popular faiths: Christianity, Islam, Hinduism, and Buddhism. By contrast, since the first century, the collective evolution of these four subsequent religions has led to the social, economic, and academic advancement of most of the Western world, (based on 2021 statistics):[6]

Christianity:[7]	2.3 billion	48 state or preferred religions
Islam:[8]	1.8 billion	27 state or preferred religions
Hinduism:[9]	1.1 billion	9 state or preferred religions
Buddhism:[10]	488 million	7 state or preferred religions

Some Christian scholars point to a time in the future to justify Jesus's remarks as a means of laying the groundwork along a twenty-century-long path for Judaism to recognize its place as needing redemption from the fall of man—just like the rest of the Gentile world, but restored (to a point), in 1947, when the United Nations granted a strip of Palestine for the establishment of a Jewish state—the first in more than 2,000 years.

> Thus said the Lord God: . . . you, O mountains of Israel, shall yield your produce and bear your fruit for My people Israel, for their

6. https://www.theguardian.com/world/2017/oct/03/more-than-20-percent-countries-have-official-state-religions-pew-survey
7. https://www.pewresearch.org/fact-tank/2017/04/05/christians-remain-worlds-largest-religious-group-but-they-are-declining-in-europe/
8. https://en.wikipedia.org/wiki/History_of_Islam
9. https://en.wikipedia.org/wiki/Hinduism_by_country
10. https://en.wikipedia.org/wiki/Buddhism

> return is near. For I will care for you: I will turn to you, and you shall be tilled and sown. I will settle a large population on you, the whole House of Israel; the towns shall be resettled, and the ruined sites rebuilt. I will multiply men and beasts upon you, and they shall increase and be fertile, and I will resettle you as you were formerly, and will make you more prosperous than you were at first. And you shall know that I am the Lord. (Ezekiel 36)

Academic research may also suggest, however, that Christ will establish His kingdom restored in the geographical region known as Jerusalem and that those who were from the descendants of Israel will be sustained as part of His sanctuary, as was foreseen in an earlier chapter from Ezekiel's writings:

> I will make a covenant of peace with them; it shall be an everlasting covenant with them: and I will place them, and multiply them, and will set my sanctuary in the midst of them for evermore. My tabernacle also shall be with them: yea, I will be their God, and they shall be my people. (Ezekiel 27)

The state located in the former Palestine notwithstanding, some scholars are not so sure the nation of Israel applies to a literal place or people,[11] given the idea of being adopted into God's family through the Atonement and Resurrection, which further suggests that the time of the Gentiles might imply a time of redemption for everyone else, as declared by Paul to the faithful of Rome, and to the Ephesians, respectively:

> Ye have received the Spirit of adoption, whereby we cry, Abba, Father. . . . Having predestinated us unto the adoption of children by Jesus Christ to himself, according to the good pleasure of his will, to the praise of the glory of his grace, wherein he hath made us accepted in the beloved. . . . That in the dispensation of the fulness of times he might gather together in one all things in Christ,

---

11. https://rsc.byu.edu/archived/volume-6-number-3-2005/adoption-and-atonement-becoming-sons-and-daughters-christ

both which are in heaven, and which are on earth; even in him. (Romans 8; Ephesians 1)

While historians and scholars may disagree on the physical location of where exactly the Lord will return and make His final stand against the wickedness of the world, all agree that the time of redemption is near—whether for Jew or Gentile.

So, is this the time of the Gentiles, and is that time coming to a close?

For many spiritual pilgrims who find themselves on their journey for truth and further knowledge about the state of the human race, the news, the political turmoil, the pandemic, and the uncertainty of economics may be considered in the immortal words of early American Thomas Paine, "a time that tries men's souls."

Let's see what we can find as we begin our own exploration.

Chapter One
Their Everlasting Confusion

"Therefore, my persecutors shall stumble, and they shall not prevail: they shall be greatly ashamed; for they shall not prosper: their everlasting confusion shall never be forgotten. . . . If the world hate you, ye know that it hated me before it hated you."

—Jeremiah 20; John 15

When attempting to organize an entire book to focus on the fate of mankind, by mapping our inevitable destiny to a smattering of historical and religious references, it's probably a good idea to fasten such concepts and suppositions on the notion that "God told me so."

Yeah, that's not confusing.

Okay, so, here's the idea: whenever any major monumental or historical event has come to pass, more often than not, there follows some form of divine prophecy[1] or intervention.

Speaking of "their everlasting confusion," let's consider our calendar,[2] for example. The way our world organizes and schedules

---

1. https://www.ligonier.org/learn/devotionals/divine-prophecy/
2. http://www.history.com/news/6-things-you-may-not-know-about-the-gregorian-calendar

the very timelines of the human race is tied to the birth of Jesus Christ. But that has been a point of contention over the years as well as a generous portion of confusion. Measuring time has been a concept that has migrated from a caprice of religious folklore to the general standard across most of modern civilization. But the idea of organizing our cycles of activities into days, weeks, months, and years (beyond the number of full moons or fall harvests) is a relatively young concept in comparison to the epoch of time. (Only since the 1700s has the current calendar been considered a "standard" measurement for periods of time). And the idea wasn't consistent from culture to culture (and still isn't). There were Icelandic calendars, Hindu calendars, Chinese calendars, Zoroastrian calendars, and (even now) Jewish calendars. And none of them agree on days, months, and years.

Since the Bronze Age, tribes, territories, cultures, and countries have been plotting cycles of time to map their respective needs, based on the movement of the moon, sun, stars, and tides. For more than a millennium, from the time Julius Caesar reformed the Roman calendar in 65 BC until the Persians established a new way of measuring time in 1079, people grew "old" a lot faster. The Julian calendar included only ten months, which stood for more than 1,000 years, until the Persians devised that a standard year lasted 365.24 days.

Although they were on to something (but not yet accurately so), the scholars of Julius Caesar's court calculated that the solar year, which was based on the two equinoxes, was drifting ever so slowly.

Following the third century and Emperor Constantine's Council at Nicaea, a debate ensued over when the rising population of Christians under a new Roman emperor would recognize the date of their Lord's resurrection from the tomb (Easter) and to address this so-called "subtle drift in the timeline."

Fast-forward through the Dark Ages, passing twelve popes named Gregory, and we come to 1582 and Gregory XIII, who set out to make revisions to the standard calendar to more accurately determine the sacred Christian holiday.

After much debate, deliberation, and a few fine-tunings to February under the direction of the Church, the Gregorian calendar became the global standard.[3] The Gregorian calendar added a small fraction of time to the 365.24, requiring an added day every fourth year to keep the timelines in sync with the sun. How ironic that the whole thing was based on when the world would be able to schedule a date to recognize the Christian namesake's triumph over death!

The idea of recognizing the birth, life, death, and resurrection of Jesus has become something of an accepted condition, which one-third of this world's population accepts: There was a God, He lived 2,000 years ago, and our world was forever changed because of His time as a man upon the earth.

But just as was predicted by those ancient prophets and kings of the Old Testament, He who would ransom Himself for the fate of mankind came into the world, and upon His birth framed the very nature of time immemorial, changing the world and forever, the way we measure time: "For I am God, and there is none else; I am God, and there is none like me, declaring the end from the beginning" (Isaiah 46:9–10).

With more than 300 references in the Old Testament foretelling the coming of the Messiah, and (just as Isaiah foresaw in chapter 53,[4] more than 700 years earlier), in a small outpost community of the ancient Roman empire, in a land where people were coerced to worship a host of characters, young Yeshua ben Youssef[5] was born into a world of tribal tumult, political unrest, and cultural captivity.

Similar to how the measurement of time itself was modified to be measured by a single, consistent standard across all cultures, the emergence of a global cultural icon would also change forever the way people considered their relationship with God.

> I will proceed to do a marvelous work among this people, even a marvelous work and a wonder: for the wisdom of their wise men shall perish, and the understanding of their prudent men shall be hid. . . . Surely your turning of things upside down shall be

---

3. https://www.britannica.com/topic/Gregorian-calendar
4. https://www.kingjamesbibleonline.org/Isaiah-Chapter-53/
5. http://www.hope-of-israel.org/messiahsname.html

> esteemed as the potter's clay: for shall the work say of him that made it, He made me not?...The meek also shall increase their joy in the Lord, and the poor among men shall rejoice in the Holy One of Israel. (Isaiah 29:14)

That a wandering teacher from the deserts of Galilee could sway even the Jews to rethink their religious position was seemed as a passing fad by many Romans, but as their collective voice grew, the rising tide of the Christian undercurrent forced even the Jews to rethink their station. And thus, with the capture and execution of Jesus and His perceived coconspirators ("Apostles"), continuing with Jeremiah's foreshadowing words of "everlasting confusion," the Christian persecution began:

> And we toil, working with our own hands; when we are reviled, we bless; when we are persecuted, we endure . . . but to the degree that you share the sufferings of Christ, keep on rejoicing, so that also at the revelation of His glory you may rejoice with exultation . . . but if anyone suffers as a Christian, he is not to be ashamed, but is to glorify God in this name. (1 Corinthians 4; 1 Peter 4)

The Roman Empire was not completely without civility, however. The three major cities of Rome, Alexandria (in Egypt), and Antioch (in Syria) were social hot spots during the early centuries of the first millennium. They were also large centers of Jewish culture, which had become highly influential in maintaining self-governing control over their territory and were natural attractions to raise up new Christian congregations.

The rising tide of faithful to follow this Jesus of Nazareth did not sit well with the local governments of the empire or the traditional Jews of the Sanhedrin (the supreme legislative council of the ancient Jews). While the empire was tossing Caesars like a salad (it saw more than a dozen within sixty years), the spreading social and religious ties to the newfound "gospel" began to extend even beyond Rome's borders, as was foretold by Jesus, Peter, and Paul in his letter to the faithful in Corinth:

> For we stretch not ourselves beyond our measure, as though we reached not unto you: for we are come as far as to you also in preaching the gospel of Christ. . . . To preach the gospel in the regions beyond you, and not to boast in another man's line of things made ready to our hand. But he that glorieth, let him glory in the Lord. (2 Corinthians 10)

But the Caesars were always looking over their shoulders, which was the case when the Sanhedrin ordered James the Just thrown from the pinnacle of the temple and clubbed to death. Rome's reaction was swift and firm, resulting in a total occupation of Jerusalem. Roman leadership, it seemed, didn't like uprisings from anyone, even if it was between heretical religious factions opposed to the state religion.

Like the children of Israel before them, the rising tide of Christianity became the favorite target of the Roman Empire.

Despite the persecution, however, the Church continued under the authority of Peter, who was given the keys of authority by Jesus, prior to Christ's ascension. Peter held those keys until his death in Rome in AD 66.

The Roman leaders always had spies plugged into the most fashionable regions of their social network—like those associated with James and his rising tide of followers, Rome's reaction was swift and firm, resulting in a total occupation of Jerusalem and Roman leadership. Religious factions and those who would offer dissenting views of Rome's divine emperor were put down quickly (or at least attempts to do so were ongoing). For the Roman leaders, the big prize in their pursuits was capturing one or more of the twelve coconspirators of the leader of this new movement, which were referred to as "apostles."[6] With the exception of John and Judas, all of Jesus's original Apostles met with terrible demise at the hands of their captors.[7]

While no one is absolutely certain, based on recorded accounts from the time, the following illustrates the fate of the original Twelve Apostles of Jesus. Each of the original twelve men called by Jesus,

---

6. https://www.christian-history.org/death-of-james.html
7. https://www.christianity.com/church/church-history/timeline/1-300/whatever-happened-to-the-twelve-apostles-11629558.html

with the exception of Judas Iscariot and John the Beloved, was summarily hunted down throughout the empire, and either murdered on the spot, or made part of a public execution.[8]

Apostle	Cause of Death/Approximate Year
Judas Iscariot	Driven by guilt, committed suicide by hanging, 34
Bartholomew	Beaten, crucified, and beheaded, 52
Phillip	Crucified at Heirapole Phryga, 52
Thomas	Impaled by lance while preaching in the East Indies (some accounts say he was in India), 52
Matthew	Killed by sword in Ethiopia, 60
James (son of Alphaeus)	Crucified in Egypt, 60
James (brother of John)	Beheaded by command of Herod, 64
Simon Peter	Crucified head down on a hill outside Rome, 66
Thaddaeus	Shot in Arafat by Roman soldiers, 72
Andrew	Bound and crucified in Greece by order of the Governor, 74
Simon Zelotes	Crucified in Persia, 74
John the Beloved	Banished to the island of Patmos, 96

Although there are many recorded interpretations on the actual method of death, what is important is that these men all died for their holy cause, while John the Beloved was banished to the island of Patmos in AD 96.[9]

By the close of the first century, the holy apostleship, under the divine authority granted to them by Christ, vanished from the earth. With the last apostles rounded up and executed, the Church no longer

---

8. https://www.bibleinfo.com/en/questions/who-were-twelve-disciples
9. http://answersfromthebook.net/was-the-apostle-john-exiled-to-the-isle-of-patmos-if-so-who-exiled-him-and-why/

had direct leadership, and many men became self-appointed leaders. Consequently, religious chapters that were organized by the likes of Stephen, James, Timothy, and Paul were left to their own designs and influences of the local cultures.

Meanwhile, in the capital city, around AD 69, and about a year before the second temple of Jerusalem was destroyed and four years after the Great Fire, Roman emperor Vespasian commissioned a massive colosseum to be constructed in the center of the thriving capital, along the Via Sacra. His son, Titus, later completed the edifice, and its use as an entertainment center has been well documented. On average, during its first year of operation, a man, woman, or child was offered up in sport and killed every five minutes around the clock. Whether part of some organized mock-battle, animal-to-man conflict, or outright public execution, the killings extended for nearly three centuries! From AD 64 until the Edict of Milan[10] in 313, in which an official proclamation ended the persecution of Christians by official decree, blood and anguish flowed from the Colosseum.

Those poor souls who believed in God came under such intense scrutiny by those who didn't that, like the children of Israel, the Christian world was almost bled, beaten, and burned out of existence. Throughout history, the faithful followers of the Man from Galilee have been ridiculed, pursued, chastised, and even rounded up and slaughtered for the entertainment of others:

> Nero substituted as culprits, and punished with the utmost refinements of cruelty, a class of men, loathed for their vices, whom the crowd styled Christians. Christus, the founder of the name, had undergone the death penalty in the reign of Tiberius, by sentence of the procurator Pontius Pilatus, and the pernicious superstition was checked for a moment, only to break out once more, not merely in Judaea, the home of the disease, but in the capital itself, where all things horrible or shameful in the world collect and find a vogue... they were covered with wild beasts' skins and torn to death by dogs; or they were fastened on crosses, and, when daylight failed were

---

10. https://www.britannica.com/topic/Edict-of-Milan

> burned to serve as lamps by night. Nero had offered his Gardens for the spectacle, and gave an exhibition in his Circus, mixing with the crowd in the habit of a charioteer, or mounted on his car. (Annals of Tacitus [AD 109])

Rome saw that the religious faction rising out of the Middle East would continue to threaten (and possibly overtake) their own deity. Even Jupiter himself—the supreme god of the ancient Romans—was cast into the shadow of this Christian God.[11] This did not sit well in the high senate and ruling Roman families. It was one thing to debate politics in the Senate, but it was a far different thing to incite sedition. And as with the Jews before, it was now the Christians who found themselves under the captor's lash. Rome was not prepared for mass conversion (yet), and in one account, the first-century bishop of the Christian church in Smyrna, Polycarp, was accused of and condemned for heresy against the empire. His crime: refusing to light a candle to recognize the Roman emperor as being above God in stature.[12]

The condemned bishop documented his last days of captivity by the Romans before being burned and stabbed:

> One might almost say that all that had gone before happened in order that the Lord might show to us from above a martyrdom in accordance with the Gospel. For he waited to be betrayed as Jesus had done, that we too might become his imitators, not thinking of ourselves alone, but also of our neighbours. And the governor said: "I have wild beasts. I will send you to them, unless you repent." And he said: "Call for them, for repentance from better to worse is not allowed us; but it is good to change from evil to righteousness." And the governor said again to him: "I will cause you to be consumed by fire, if you not scared by the beasts, unless you repent." But Polycarp said: "You threaten with the fire that burns for a time and is quickly quenched, for you do not know the fire which awaits the wicked in the judgment to come and in everlasting punishment.

---

11. https://en.wikipedia.org/wiki/Persecution_of_Christians_in_the_Roman_Empire
12. https://www.christianitytoday.com/history/people/martyrs/polycarp.html

> But why are you waiting? Come, do what you will." (Acts of Thecla and Paul [AD 155])[13]

Greek philosophies[14] and other local customs became stronger influences among the Christian factions. By the close of the second century, there were house churches and Christian spin-offs covering almost every major region of the empire. Some efforts were made to keep the foundation of the Church intact, the most notable being that of Ignatius of Antioch[15] in about AD 110, but even his efforts were made while he was on his way to his own execution in Rome:

> Let me be food for the wild beasts, for they are my way to God. I am God's wheat and shall be ground by their teeth so that I may become Christ's pure bread. Pray to Christ for me that the animals will be the means of making me a sacrificial victim for God. No earthly pleasures, no kingdoms of this world can benefit me in any way. . . . The prince of this world is determined to lay hold of me and to undermine my will which is intent on God. Let none of you here help him; instead show yourselves on my side, which is also God's side. Do not talk about Jesus Christ as long as you love this world. Do not harbor envious thoughts. And supposing I should see you, if then I should beg you to intervene on my behalf, do not believe what I say. (Ignatius of Antioch [AD 107])

The "Church," as it was organized by Christ and further established by the Apostles throughout the lands, fell deeper into a state of endless confusion and segregation, which some religious scholars would suggest has lasted nearly 2,000 years:

> The Christian churches in the absence of revelation had tightened their views protectively defensively either around a holy man the

---

13. https://pressbooks.bccampus.ca/spectaclesintheromanworldsourcebook/chapter/executions-of-christians/
14. https://www.gospeltruth.net/gkphilo.htm
15. https://www.christianitytoday.com/history/people/martyrs/ignatius-of-antioch.html

> pope and hierarchy or around a holy book the bible which was alleged to be all sufficient and only sufficient religious knowing came only through that word and all other claims were treated as emotional extravagance. . . . There is new recognition that the word mysteries as it appears in the new testament and in its background literature means something more something one can reach through with knowledge or gnosis not simply on the ground of faith which was the protestant claim but with knowledge. It has been terrifying to men in charge of men s souls to be so bereft they now recognize that while damning prophets they themselves have been cast in the role for any man at any time to say if you will do so and so you will be saved is to make prophecy it is either true or false and suddenly the recognition comes that Christ did not say there would be no prophets that would have been a categorical way of enabling Christians to avoid deception instead he gave tests for distinguishing the true from the false. (Truman G. Madsen[16])

Early writings found in the Old and New Testaments suggest that the intersection between God's favoring the Jews and His turning to the Gentile nations for their redemption set in motion a series of global evolutionary events that have continued to serve as both unifier as well as disrupter for cultures and faiths all around the world for 2,000 years.

"Everlasting confusion," indeed!

---

16. https://scholarsarchive.byu.edu/cgi/viewcontent.cgi?article=1689&context=byusq

Chapter Two
In the Sight of the Beast

"And he exerciseth all the power of the first beast before him, and causeth the earth and them which dwell therein to worship the first beast, whose deadly wound was healed. And he doeth great wonders, so that he maketh fire come down from heaven on the earth in the sight of men, And deceiveth them that dwell on the earth by the means of those miracles which he had power to do in the sight of the beast; saying to them that dwell on the earth, that they should make an image to the beast, which had the wound by a sword, and did live. And he had power to give life unto the image of the beast, that the image of the beast should both speak, and cause that as many as would not worship the image of the beast should be killed."

—Revelation 13

Rounding up Christians and using them for political firewood became something of a trend throughout the first century and beyond. The axiom that "politics or religion don't mix" was no truer than among the halls of the Roman leadership after the death of Christ. Rule and expansion of the empire under the Caesars left little wiggle room for philosophies or beliefs that might have been contrary to the status quo. And speaking of "Beasts," Rome took less than a century to kill off the Apostles and their chief troublemaker (Jesus). By the third century, Christianity was practiced only by those who would dare risk the chances of being captured and offered up in some beastly or bloody sport within the Colosseum.[1]

Based on its Latin root, *religio*, which means "something that binds," the religion of the time, similar to today, was based on a few basic tenets: God spoke to somebody; somebody felt appointed by God to speak to somebody else about God; somebody else told everybody else, and everyone began worshipping God based on the influence. Trust and confidence that the first person or group was in touch with divine authority, or until somebody new came into town (sounds like the makings of a good song!)[2] were the precepts to starting up a new worship service.

Devotion to the Roman gods was not the only fashionable measure of faith in the empire during the first century. Jewish communities had been part of the Roman landscape for centuries, and eventually it led to conflict that saw the destruction of the Jewish temple, as mentioned in the prior chapter. Further persecution and dissolution of the children of Israel fractured into numerous religious sects, and they too became a favorite sport of the Roman hunt for heretics. In 66 AD, Florus, Roman governor of Judea, slaughtered everyone he could find in the Jewish market for hurling insults at him. A full-scale rebellion of Judea resulted in several Roman legions attacking the countryside to put down any potential uprising. In his account, Jewish high priest and chronicler Flavius Josephus (whose Jewish name was Yosef ben Matityahu) wrote of the slaughter of 40,000 Jews by Vespasian and his Roman legions:

> From one end of Galilee to the other there was an orgy of fire and bloodshed; no horror, no calamity was spared. (Flavius Josephus)[3]

---

1. http://www.tribunesandtriumphs.org/colosseum/colosseum-christian-martyrs.htm
2. https://americansongwriter.com/new-kid-in-town-the-eagles-behind-the-song/
3. https://www.ccel.org/ccel/josephus/works/files/works.html

From the days of Noah to today, religious factions from all over the spectrum of Judeo-Christian history have been claiming they were the God's favored family:

> And Jesus answered and said unto them, Take heed that no man deceive[s] you. For many shall come in my name, saying, I am Christ; and shall deceive many. . . . And many false prophets shall rise and shall deceive many. (Matthew 24)

The idea of somewhat autonomous understandings of God and His ministry on the earth had become so widespread in the first and second centuries that the Apostle Paul—a Jewish convert to Christianity—dedicated his life to cautioning the faithful followers of Christ to stay close to the word and doctrine and to remain consistent in their practices of keeping the faith:

> For ye are all the children of God by faith in Christ Jesus. . . . There is neither Jew nor Greek, there is neither bond nor free, there is neither male nor female: for ye are all one in Christ Jesus. (Galatians 3)

The land masses that border the Mediterranean Sea are vast. For centuries, the cities along the Mediterranean depended on sea travel, and for the Apostle Paul and his colleagues—including Luke and Timothy—keeping an eye on the growing Christian faith meant travel by boat to the many communities. As they traveled through each new venue, Paul discovered variations of Jesus's teachings—even including independent writings and random ideas about the nature of God and angels. But Paul didn't agree with what he found. His letters, as documented in the books of the New Testament, reveal how he worked to establish a single stream of thought despite the vast differences between tribes and towns:

> Forasmuch as ye are manifestly declared to be the epistle of Christ ministered by us, written not with ink, but with the Spirit of the living God; not in tables of stone, but in fleshy tables of the heart . . . who also hath made us able ministers of the new testament; not of

the letter, but of the spirit: for the letter killeth, but the spirit giveth life. (2 Corinthians 3)

Just as communities today develop based on unique cultural, social, and even political ideologies, by the end of the first century, Christian sects had developed independent concepts about what was and was not permitted behavior, prompting what was left of Christ's leadership to embark on those final acts of unification.

For the Christian faithful in communities all along the Mediterranean, Paul's letters to the thirteen churches that had quietly cropped up through the empire were a way of maintaining consistency amid the disputing factions who began creating their own followings and interpretations of Christianity almost as soon as Jesus was nailed to the cross. The Bible records three significant journeys made by Paul in which he encountered a variety of churches, all of which had drifted into their own individual sets of beliefs and tribulations.

The Bible includes Paul's thirteen letters, although scholars still debate the authenticity of his being the author of Hebrews. In all, the various sects of the ancient Christian faith included many towns and congregations, each with their own ideologies. While not a definitive list, the following suggests some of the major populations where Christianity found itself in one form or other mingled with the local traditions and customs, and which were center to Paul's three missionary journeys:

- **Antioch:**[4] The first reference to followers of Jesus as "Christians," the so-called "Followers of the Way," were the first Gentile converts to assemble as a formal congregation.
- **Assos:**[5] A community of intellects, where logic and facts superseded the notion of a risen Messiah. Assos was the birthplace and home to the school founded by ancient philosopher Aristotle.

---

4. https://www.ligonier.org/learn/devotionals/the-church-in-antioch/
5. http://bibleatlas.org/assos.htm

- **Athens:**[6] Classified as a "Free City" by the empire, Athens was heavily influenced by traditional Greek philosophy.
- **Caesarea:**[7] Blended Roman religion, with Jewish hard-liners who were killed for their faith.
- **Corinth:**[8] Also influenced by Greece's Olympian gods, which included what Christian scholars often refer to as "moral corruption."[9]
- **Cyprus:**[10] Greek religious exiles that congregated and worshipped in caves, were taught how to worship by Barnabas.
- **Ephesus:**[11] Worshipped the resident "Mother Goddess Artemis" and a blend of Jewish influence with Gentile converts.
- **Iconium:**[12] Greek-Asian influence blended with Judaism.
- **Jerusalem:** Where three distinct groups of Jews (Palestinians,[13] Rabbinics,[14] and Hellenists).[15]
- **Laodicea[16] (Collose)**: The last of the seven churches referenced by John in his Revelation, the faithful there were said to have been founded by a student of Paul's, whose congregations loved their wealth more than God and followed dynastic rule and traditional Roman myth.
- **Miletus:**[17] Ancient Indo-Asian city that practiced various distorted forms of paganism mingled with Christian fundamentals.

---

6. https://www.ancient.eu/Greek_Religion/
7. https://www.britannica.com/place/Caesarea
8. http://bibleatlas.org/corinth.htm
9. https://bbhchurchconnection.wordpress.com/2015/01/09/how-immoral-was-corinth-really/
10. http://ringofchrist.com/early-christian-history/
11. https://www.ancient.eu/ephesos/
12. http://www.biblestudy.org/apostlepaul/life-epistles-of-apostle-paul/iconium-lystra-derbe.html
13. https://www.theatlantic.com/magazine/archive/1919/07/a-jewish-palestine/303393/
14. https://www.thegospelcoalition.org/article/9-things-you-should-know-about-rabbinic-judaism/
15. http://www.jewishencyclopedia.com/articles/7535-hellenism
16. https://www.biblicalarchaeology.org/daily/biblical-sites-places/biblical-archaeology-sites/church-of-laodicea-in-the-bible-and-archaeology/
17. https://www.thoughtco.com/miletus-greek-history-119714

- **Philippi:**[18] A Roman stronghold with its own gold mine, included a large population of Italian settlers.
- **Rome:**[19] In the first century, Roman religion was a house-to-house principle that centered around whoever was the traditional god worshipped by the head of the house.
- **Samaria:**[20] Opposed repatriation of Judah to the northern lands, call themselves the "Keepers of the Torah."
- **Thessalonica:**[21] An ancient port city whose local parishioners mixed their new Christian faith with traditional immoral practices of mysticism tied to idols ("Cabiri").[22]
- **Troas:**[23] A port city on the Aegean Sea, popular for Roman cult following, paganism, and typical port-side debauchery of the times.

The formal religion of ancient Romans[24] was all about binding families to households, households to the male dominant figure, and binding him to his favorite deity. Such was the way of Roman worship and it was indisputable.

By the beginning of the fourth century, Rome became unmanageable from a single point of view, and by empirical decree of the emperor Diocletian, four lesser kings assisted the empire in holding off the barbarian hordes from the north (the Goths, Vandals, and so on). The tetrarchy,[25] as it was known, was not very successful, and within a few years, everybody wanted to be the sole leader over the vast Mediterranean empire.

Then something happened on the way to the Forum.

---

18. https://www.ancient.eu/Philippi/
19. http://www.mcgill.ca/classics/files/classics/2006-7-07.pdf
20. http://www.bible.ca/archeology/bible-archeology-samaritans.htm
21. https://www.biblestudytools.com/history/joseph-barber-lightfoot-biblical-essays/the-church-of-thessalonica.html
22. https://www.encyclopedia.com/philosophy-and-religion/ancient-religions/ancient-religion/cabiri
23. https://bibleatlas.org/troas.htm
24. https://www.ancient.eu/Roman_Religion/
25. https://courses.lumenlearning.com/suny-hccc-worldhistory/chapter/diocletian-and-the-tetrarchy/

By the start of the fourth century, the military campaigns of Constantine resulted in unifying the four regions of Rome, which had formerly been divided into lesser realms. A man whose mother had converted to Christianity, Constantine was the first Roman emperor to not only declare Christianity absolved from further exploit and persecution. Upon adopting Christianity as the preferred religion of the court, Constantine moved the seat of the empire to a port town near the mouth of the Black Sea in 324, where traditional Eastern Europe meets West. The ancient city of Byzantium was renamed Constantinople. The seeds of what would become the Great Schism between the Greek Orthodox and Roman Catholicism were planted, taking 700 years to germinate.[26]

Today, there are more than 4,300 different religions practiced in the world,[27] with more than 33,000 independent Christian sects, fulfilling a common theme among the Lord and his followers about the last days:

> Beloved, believe not every spirit, but try the spirits whether they are of God: because many false prophets are gone out into the world. . . . Every spirit that confesseth that Jesus Christ is come in the flesh is of God: And every spirit that confesseth not that Jesus Christ is come in the flesh is not of God: and this is that spirit of antichrist, whereof ye have heard that it should come; and even now already is it in the world. (1 John 4)

Just as was advised by Paul, John, and others, during His mortal ministry, Jesus warned of those who would try to sway the faithful into thinking they were directed by Him—or that they were Jesus Himself, returned as foretold by the ancient prophets. In Matthew, the writer records Jesus as saying many will come to deceive and that they "will hear of wars and rumors of wars."[28] Christian tradition

26. https://www.britannica.com/topic/Christianity/The-Schism-of-1054
27. https://www.theregister.co.uk/2006/10/06/the_odd_body_religion/
28. https://abn.churchofjesuschrist.org/study/manual/gospel-topics/war?lang=eng&abVersion=V01&abName=GLOB88

refers to the "Great Tribulation"[29] as a time mentioned by Jesus as being a period of perpetual unrest—in society, in families, and in the hearts of men.

For the faithful of Christ, Paul, in his letter to the Christians in Corinth, testified that God is not a God of confusion:

> If therefore the whole church come together into one place, and all speak with tongues, and there come in those that are unlearned, or unbelievers, will they not say that ye are mad? . . . For God is not the author of confusion, but of peace, as in all churches of the saints. (1 Corinthians 14)

Listening to those whom Jesus designated as His mouthpiece, and retaining a fundamental understanding of His gospel, allows all cultures to rely on what some religious leaders may consider to be the "common denominator" of faith in the principles of heaven, regardless of who happens to be ruling the landscape down here on earth.

29. https://lifehopeandtruth.com/prophecy/revelation/great-tribulation/

Chapter Three
Thou Shalt Not Serve Other Gods

"But it shall come to pass, if thou wilt not hearken unto the voice of the Lord thy God, to observe to do all his commandments and his statutes which I command thee this day; that all these curses shall come upon thee, and overtake thee: . . . The Lord shall bring thee, and thy king which thou shalt set over thee, unto a nation which neither thou nor thy fathers have known; and there shalt thou serve other gods, wood and stone."

—Deuteronomy 28

DISOBEDIENCE CAN HAVE PAINFUL CONSEQUENCES.

From the days of their wanderings in the desert, during their captivity by the Assyrians, Babylonians, and Egyptians, when they were "occupied" by the Roman Empire, all the way to the time preceding the twentieth century, the children of Israel have been considered God's collective problem child:

> The Lord shall bring a nation against thee from far, from the end of the earth, as swift as the eagle flieth; a nation whose tongue thou shalt not understand; A nation of fierce countenance, which shall not regard the person of the old, nor shew favour to the young: . . . And he shall besiege thee in all thy gates, until thy high and fenced walls come down, wherein thou trustedst, throughout all thy land: and he shall besiege thee in all thy gates throughout all thy land, which the Lord thy God hath given thee. (Deuteronomy 28)

The domination and persecution of the Jewish nation has been a consistent problem for Israel since the legendary times of Moses, when, after he led what was left of his people out of Egypt, they set the tone for what would be thousands of years of oppression by just about every other nation throughout the history of the world. But God warned them time and again that their disobedience, lack of faith, and wanton turning to worldly idols would get them into mortal trouble:

> Among those nations you shall find no rest, and there will be no resting place for the sole of your foot; but there the Lord will give you a trembling heart, failing of eyes, and despair of soul. . . . Now the generation to come, your sons who rise up after you and the foreigner who comes from a distant land, when they see the plagues of the land and the diseases with which the Lord has afflicted it, will say, all its land is brimstone and salt, a burning waste. . . . You, however, I will scatter among the nations and will draw out a sword after you, as your land becomes desolate, and your cities become waste. (Leviticus 26; Deuteronomy 28)

Generations of prophets have written, sung, and spoken regarding God's admonitions to His children. On numerous occasions, Israel had been warned that they would be cast among the peoples of the world if they did not remain faithful to God's covenants with them. The Jews were advised repeatedly that they would be dispersed worldwide if they were not faithful to their covenant with God:

> If thou wilt not hearken unto the voice of the Lord thy God, to observe to do all his commandments and his statutes which I command thee this day; that all these curses shall come upon thee, and overtake thee: Cursed shalt thou be in the city, and cursed shalt thou be in the field. . . . The Lord shall send upon thee cursing, vexation, and rebuke, in all that thou settest thine hand unto for to do, until thou be destroyed, and until thou perish quickly; because of the wickedness of thy doings, whereby thou hast forsaken me. (Deuteronomy 28)

The witnesses of Christ's mission and ministry, as documented in the first century in the writings of Matthew, Mark, Peter, James, John, Paul, and Timothy, were authored and compiled before the end of the second century and became known as the Novum Testamentum,[1] or "Renewed Covenant." This compiled volume of letters and manuscripts became sort of a post-Hebrew-centered discourse on the ideologies surrounding the early Christian movement and conversion from Judaism, and ultimately became a compilation of twenty-seven individual writings compiled by Erasmus into a body of work, which Christians now refer to as the New Testament.[2]

The contrast in cultural consciousness, however, rested on the fact that Paul's letters to the Christian faithful, as well as to the Hebrews, had limited exposure but just enough to get him and those faithful to the new sect into more trouble than would otherwise befall them. Few people of Jewish faith even knew of the tale of a Risen Messiah, and as a result, further perpetuated the speculation by Christians, Hellenists, and Gentiles, that not only did the Jews kill their own leader, but they also cared little to learn more about any so-called plan of redemption for them.

Europe was no friendlier to the Jewish culture. In the final years of the seventh century, French and Spanish edict forced Jewish families to convert to Catholicism or be enslaved.[3] Such actions, from

1. http://journals.sagepub.com/doi/abs/10.1177/2051677016628242
2. http://www.helsinki.fi/teol/pro/_merenlah/oppimateriaalit/text/english/newtest.htm
3. https://www.economist.com/news/europe/21596963-offer-right-past-wrong-may-not-lead-huge-influx-people-1492-and-all

the outside, suggest they were based on religious bias between the Christian majority and the Jewish minority, although historians suggest that the continued persecution of Judaism as a whole was born out of a combination of political, economic, and ideological bias.[4]

By 1095, when Pope Urban II called the first crusade as being the will of God, both Christian and Jewish communities were scattered throughout Europe and the Mediterranean region. Despite the new Christian doctrine of "love thy neighbor," neither side would find such doctrine favorable, and again, the dominating force would prey on the weaker side, even though they were merely a misunderstood faction between Christianity and Islam—the real target of the Crusades:

> What is the good of going to the end of the world at great loss of men and money to fight the Saracens [Muslims], when we permit among us other infidels who are a thousand times more guilty towards Christ than [Islam]? (Hugh, Abbot of Cluny [~1095])[5]

Throughout the German region of the Rhine and into present-day Czech Republic, Christian crusaders raided towns and pillaged Jewish families. In the early summer of 1096, more than 900 Jewish victims fell under sword, knife, and hoof of the Christian crusaders—much of their journeys to the Holy Land being funded by their plunders on Jewish families. It would seem that the words found in Luke were coming to pass—even 1,000 years after his original testimony:

> And ye shall be betrayed both by parents, and brethren, and kinsfolks, and friends; and some of you shall they cause to be put to death. . . . And when ye shall see Jerusalem compassed with armies, then know that the desolation thereof is nigh. . . . And they shall fall by the edge of the sword, and shall be led away captive into all nations: and Jerusalem shall be trodden down of the Gentiles, until the times of the Gentiles be fulfilled. (Luke 21)

---

4. https://www.ushmm.org/wlc/en/article.php?ModuleId=10005175
5. https://www.catholicireland.net/saintoftheday/st-hugh-1024-1109-abbot-of-cluny/

For the next thousand years, Judaism was hunted throughout Europe as the political target for all sorts of censuring, rancor, and persecution, especially during the period known as the Crusades, when traveling bands of Christian knights would often exercise their superior fighting prowess on Jewish communities along their route to the Holy Land.[6]

Then came the twentieth century.

By 1920, Austria, Germany, and Switzerland were home to the majority of the house of Israel, which was essentially a people without a country. After the failure of the Weimar Republic[7]—a Jewish-influenced initiative to save Germany from economic ruin—and a Great War that left more than 6 million Germans dead or wounded, the nation of Germany fell into a collapsed society trapped by a failed monarchy.

Like so many times throughout history, the downtrodden and repressed population of the majority turned their hatred toward a favorite scapegoat of history: the crestfallen children of Israel. Based on their failed policies and excessive compensations agreed to in the Treaty of Versailles after World War I, and with total economic collapse looming throughout the hinterland, when even the German middle class found themselves in abject poverty, the extremist fringe of the Nationalist Socialist Party came to power, and a former German army corporal named Adolph Hitler was appointed chancellor in 1933.[8]

The Jewish population's path would be forever altered with the rise of Hitler's Third Reich in Germany and Stalin's Soviet Union to the north and east. Throughout Germany the Reich ordered a segregation between Aryan (those who were of pure German descent) and non-Aryan (usually identified as Jews and gypsies). The Nuremberg Laws of 1935 made a formal edict[9] establishing Arianism as a supreme race that must be purged of all outside sources—especially the Jewish

---

6. https://www.chabad.org/library/article_cdo/aid/2617029/jewish/The-Bloody-Crusades.htm
7. https://www.history.com/topics/weimar-republic
8. https://www.history.com/this-day-in-history/adolf-hitler-is-named-chancellor-of-germany
9. https://www.ushmm.org/wlc/en/article.php?ModuleId=10005681

influence. Hitler's SS and Gestapo rounded up Jews by the millions, sending them to labor camps and often eventual death by gas chambers in camps that included Auschwitz, Treblinka, and Dachau.

The mass genocide of the Jewish nation became known as the Holocaust, and throughout the period between 1938, which began with Germany's Night of Broken Glass,[10] and the end of World War II in 1945, historical records show more than 6 million Jews were killed[11] under Hitler's orders, while millions more suffered and perished in Stalin's Gulag.[12]

Despite thousands of years of persecution, however, God promised not to forget or completely forsake his children, as prophesied by Hosea:

> For the children of Israel shall abide many days without a king, and without a prince, and without a sacrifice, and without an image, and without an ephod, and without teraphim: Afterward shall the children of Israel return, and seek the Lord their God, and David their king; and shall fear the Lord and his goodness in the latter days. (Hosea 3)

In 1948, with the stroke of a pen and the raising of a few hands in a room, the United Nations carved out of the former territory of Palestine, a strip of land between Jordan and the shores of the Mediterranean, which became the State of Israel, fulfilling (finally), biblical prophecy:[13]

> The State of Israel will be open for Jewish immigration and for the Ingathering of the Exiles; it will foster the development of the country for the benefit of all its inhabitants; it will be based on

---

10. https://www.ushmm.org/wlc/en/article.php?ModuleId=10005201
11. https://www.ushmm.org/wlc/en/article.php?ModuleId=10008193
12. https://news.stanford.edu/2010/09/23/naimark-stalin-genocide-092310/
13. https://mfa.gov.il/MFA/MFA-Archive/2003/Pages/The%20Land%20of%20Promise-%twentiethe%20State%20of%20Israel.aspx

> freedom, justice and peace as envisaged by the prophets of Israel. (Israeli Declaration of Establishment [1948])[14]

Within the first eighteen months of being established, Israel's population doubled, inviting all Jewish people to consider returning to the homeland that they believed stolen so many centuries before. Today, in a time that some religious historians have proclaimed as the coming to pass of the fulness of the Gentiles,[15] following centuries of persecution, more than 6 million people call the little strip of land between Jordan and the Mediterranean home. Israel calls to Jews throughout the world to return to ancient lands and take up residence in a long-awaited reunion that Christians have foreseen since Moses first promised his people they would someday be restored to their land:[16]

> Now it shall come to pass, when all these things come upon you, the blessing and the curse which I have set before you, and you call them to mind among all the nations where the Lord your God drives you, and you return to the Lord your God and obey His voice, according to all that I command you today, you and your children, with all your heart and with all your soul, that the Lord your God will bring you back from captivity, and have compassion on you, and gather you again from all the nations where the Lord your God has scattered you. If any of you are driven out to the farthest parts under heaven, from there the Lord your God will gather you, and from there He will bring you. (Deuteronomy 30)

A common phrase that is often sung by Jewish families during Passover services has been a common theme for nearly 600 years. For subsequent generations since the fifteenth century, "next year in Jerusalem" became almost a battle cry of hope and optimism, as there

---

14. https://www.mfa.gov.il/mfa/foreignpolicy/peace/guide/pages/declaration%20of%20establishment%20of%20state%20of%20israel.aspx
15. http://www.signstimes.com/?p=article&a=40044012100.645
16. http://www.truthnet.org/Endtimes/introduction/Signs/

had not been a Jewish occupied Jerusalem since the beginning of the Messianic Era.

Prophets of old, from Moses to Isaiah, from Luke to Paul—and even Jesus Himself—wrote of a time that has since been fulfilled, as Jerusalem once again, belongs to Israel.

Part Two
Therefore, Endure Hardness

"We knew before we were born that we were coming to the earth for bodies and experience and that we would have joys and sorrows, ease and pain, comforts and hardships, health and sickness, successes and disappointments, and we knew also that after a period of life we would die. We accepted all these eventualities with a glad heart, eager to accept both the favorable and unfavorable. We eagerly accepted the chance to come earthward even though it might be for only a day or a year. Perhaps we were not so much concerned whether we should die of disease, of accident, or of senility. We were willing to take life as it came and as we might organize and control it, and this without murmur, complaint, or unreasonable demands."

—Spencer W. Kimball,
Faith Precedes the Miracle[1]

1. https://byu.overdrive.com/media/1675160

I would believe in the concept of Christianity if I didn't know so much." We've all known someone who has tried to intellectualize the faith of others to believe in some form of religious ideology. Humility is a difficult mannerism to master. Whether spoken by a wise man or a fool, pride of station often fuels the hubris that gets in the way of faith.

For Christianity one of the many telltale signs of the times relates to a vision experienced by the ancient prophet Daniel:

> There shall be a time of trouble, such as never was since there was a nation even to that same time: and at that time thy people shall be delivered, every one that shall be found written in the book. . . . And they that be wise shall shine as the brightness of the firmament; and they that turn many to righteousness as the stars for ever and ever. . . . But thou, O Daniel, shut up the words, and seal the book, even to the time of the end: many shall run to and fro, and knowledge shall be increased. (Daniel 12)

Daniel was counseled that his prophecy's meaning would be sealed until the time of its fulfillment was near.

From the Stone Age to the Information Age, the evolution of the human race has often been marked by the advancements surrounding the things we use to make life easier. But at what cost?

Christian leaders throughout the world accept that although knowledge and the accumulation of information is growing at an exponential rate, as history has recorded, this seems to always come at a price:

> Socrates lived during the long transition from a largely oral tradition to a newer information technology consisting of writing down words and information and collecting those writings into scrolls and books. Famously Socrates was somewhat antagonistic to writing and scholars claim that he never wrote anything down himself. Socrates tells a fable of an Egyptian God he names Theuth who gives the gift of writing to a king named Thamus, [who] is not pleased with the gift and replies, "If men learn this, it will implant forgetfulness in their souls; they will cease to exercise

> memory because they rely on that which is written, calling things to remembrance no longer from within themselves, but by means of external marks." (*Stanford Encyclopedia of Philosophy*, 2012)[2]

While societies continue to improve science, principles of technology, medicine, and engineering designs, theologians suggest that a head full of knowledge with an empty heart[3] will lead society closer to the brink of its own destruction. To Daniel's prophecy, we fast-forward to the Apostle John, who was told in his vision that the time was at hand not to seal his prophecies:

> For the Lord God giveth them light: and they shall reign for ever and ever. . . . And he said unto me, These sayings are faithful and true: and the Lord God of the holy prophets sent his angel to shew unto his servants the things which must shortly be done. Behold, I come quickly: blessed is he that keepeth the sayings of the prophecy of this book. . . . And he saith unto me, Seal not the sayings of the prophecy of this book: for the time is at hand. (Revelation 22)

While both Daniel and John received similar visions of the time in which "knowledge" (rather than God), would be king, the power of the mind has never been more scrutinized than in our current age of artificial intelligence, "smart appliances," autonomous vehicles—even internet dating.

At the close of the twentieth century, noted American architect Buckminster Fuller wrote in his book, *Critical Path*, an observation that purports human knowledge doubling every 100 years, which he identified as the "Knowledge Doubling Curve."[4] Following the close of World War II, that cycle had been accelerated to every twenty-five years. Based on the current rate of growth and advancements surrounding the Internet of Things, some futurists think we are not

---

2. https://plato.stanford.edu/entries/it-moral-values/#MorChaInfTec
3. https://countdown.org/en/signs/increased-knowledge/
4. https://www.tandfonline.com/doi/full/10.1080/24735132.2020.1731203

far off from the accumulation of knowledge doubling twice within a twenty-four-hour period![5]

And then there's the debate surrounding the coming of something called a Technological Singularity, in which the invention of artificial hyper-intelligence will inadvertently initiate cascading technological growth, resulting in profound transformation in how artificial intelligence interacts with and ultimately becomes dominant over the human race.

Just how "smart" is the world getting?

The data contained online now doubles every six months.

Technical knowledge doubles every thirty-six months, while printed resources double every eight years.

By the time this book is published, more than half of the 1 million new titles planned for printing this year will have gone to press.[6]

There are more than 1.8 billion individual websites[7] (575,000 new sites every day) and more than 4.5 billion internet users.[8]

While Christian scholars infer that the knowledge denoted in Daniel's vision corresponds with that wisdom that comes through the Holy Ghost to discern the mysteries of God, the implied higher knowledge referred to in John's vision pertains to the gospel of Christ and His fulfilling the probation of mankind through the Atonement and resurrection:

> Blessed is he that readeth, and they that hear the words of this prophecy, and keep those things which are written therein: for the time is at hand. . . . And from Jesus Christ, who is the faithful witness, and the first begotten of the dead, and the prince of the kings of the earth. Unto him that loved us, and washed us from our sins in his own blood, and hath made us kings and priests unto God and his Father. . . . Behold, he cometh with clouds; and every eye shall see him, and they also which pierced him: and all kindreds of the earth shall wail because of him. (Revelation 1)

---

5. https://lodestarsolutions.com/keeping-up-with-the-surge-of-information-and-human-knowledge/
6. https://malwarwickonbooks.com/published-every-year/
7. http://www.internetlivestats.com/total-number-of-websites/
8. https://websitesetup.org/news/how-many-websites-are-there/

In a time in which the world will generate more knowledge than 57,000 Libraries of Congress within a year's time, those who may look at this as a mere humanistic advancement of man's ability to think and reason might dismiss this explosive age of knowledge as a mere caprice of evolution.[9]

Again, however, the faithful may turn to John's experience on the island of Patmos, in which he is carried in a further vision of the latter days:

> And from Jesus Christ, who is the faithful witness, and the first begotten of the dead, and the prince of the kings of the earth. Unto him that loved us, and washed us from our sins in his own blood, And hath made us kings and priests unto God and his Father; to him be glory and dominion for ever and ever. . . . Behold, he cometh with clouds; and every eye shall see him, and they also which pierced him: and all kindreds of the earth shall wail because of him. . . . I am Alpha and Omega, the beginning and the ending, saith the Lord, which is, and which was, and which is to come, the Almighty. (Revelation 1)

Only a century ago, the horse was faster than the newfangled automobile that was taking European and American society by storm. Airplanes were made out of wood and aluminum, and telegraphs were still the preferred means of mass communications. Today most people have hand-held devices that can control every aspect of their lives, send messages anywhere in the world, and store more data than what was used in the early space programs. Man, as was foretold by the Old Testament prophet Amos, has become exceedingly proficient in "wander[ing] from sea to sea, and from the north even to the east, they shall run to and fro."[10]

But to what end?

Despite those noted men and women of science, as well as math scholars and other intellectuals who acknowledge their faith being tied

---

9. https://www.industrytap.com/knowledge-doubling-every-12-months-soon-to-be-every-12-hours/3950
10. http://www.bibleone.net/Intellect-Faith.htm

to Christian principles, the general consensus—especially in light of the Information Age—is that the Christian ideology lacks physical substance and ignores the fundamental values of sound logic. The result is a suitable out that justifies not believing in anything other than what is built, produced, seen or suffered, rather than what might have been written (and foreseen), in a distant past, as recorded by Paul almost 2,000 years ago:

> Because that which may be known of God is manifest in them; for God hath shewed it unto them. For the invisible things of him from the creation of the world are clearly seen, being understood by the things that are made, even his eternal power and Godhead; so that they are without excuse: Because that, when they knew God, they glorified him not as God, neither were thankful; but became vain in their imaginations, and their foolish heart was darkened. Professing themselves to be wise, they became fools. (Romans 1)

While the agnostic side of the debate over "intellect versus religious" may wrestle that there's room for both, a surefire sign of the times is the idea that the human race is struggling more and more with the choice between being smart and growing our faith.[11]

But faith and intellect are not mutually exclusive. Those who can see both sides of the argument might suggest there's opportunity to develop both.

To exercise faith in something, the individual must first believe that the outcome will match his or her expectations in that for which faith is being exercised. For the world to believe in God, for example, which may imply suspending scientific reason for the notion that a singular being oversees the human race from some far-off place, with the promise of sending His Firstborn Son back to rule someday, a change of heart is required, while also allowing for the added perspective that "anything is possible."

---

11. https://iep.utm.edu/faith-re/

Chapter Four
The World Languisheth

"The land shall be utterly emptied, and utterly spoiled. The earth mourneth and fadeth away, the world languisheth and fadeth away. The earth also is defiled under the inhabitants thereof; because they have transgressed the laws, changed the ordinance, broken the everlasting covenant. Therefore hath the curse devoured the earth."

—Isaiah 24

"POLITICAL CORRECTNESS"

Political correctness symbolizes a distinctive mix of liberal ideology (referring to the concept that disadvantaged sections of a population should allow the more successful masses to support them),[1] combined with a sort-of puritanical idea that endorses moral oversight being a required, institutionalized guideline for a society to thrive. In the broadest term, the idea of being "PC" as it were, invokes hypersensitivity to what might be considered a ratcheting down on the color of our language.

1. https://www.britannica.com/topic/political-correctness

For example, references to physical identification (race, gender, culture, and so on) are the focal point when considering the political correctness of a description or conversation (censoring, or extreme reform for matters normally found in colloquial conversation would be subject to a PC discussion).[2]

To be politically correct, then, according to this definition, is to embrace a form of extreme inclusion for those who are socially disadvantaged. While liberal thinkers would argue that such a definition would apply to those who have been afforded fewer opportunities than others, Christian conservatives might suggest that "extreme exclusion" and "socially disadvantaged" could apply to any group depending on the circumstances.

The argument for political correctness would also suggest that taking a bias toward or against any form of governance, guidance, or leadership would be offensive—especially given the polarity that often exists between believers and non-believers.[3] History has shown that such dissention often leads to chaos, anarchy, and destruction:

> And the people shall be oppressed, everyone by another, and everyone by his neighbour: the child shall behave himself proudly against the ancient, and the base against the honourable. . . . The shew of their countenance doth witness against them; and they declare their sin as Sodom, they hide it not. Woe unto their soul! for they have rewarded evil unto themselves. (Isaiah 3)

The legend of Noah,[4] the *Epic of Gilgamesh*,[5] and Homer's *Iliad*[6] all frame the chaos of the human condition around an inherent characteristic to distrust a society that was not ruled by order and discipline, which ultimately leads to its destruction. Add to the confusion

---

2. https://www.thoughtco.com/what-is-political-correctness-4178215
3. http://christredeemerchurch.org/home/romans-8-and-the-difference-between-a-believer-and-a-non-believer/
4. https://answersingenesis.org/noahs-ark/is-noahs-ark-myth/
5. http://www.ancient-literature.com/other_gilgamesh.html
6. http://www.sparknotes.com/lit/iliad/summary/

something that has the power to impact every human on the planet, and things can change pretty quickly.

Political correctness aside, modern prophets and religious scholars may suggest that all it takes to humble a people is something like a pandemic as a means of level-setting society. President Russell M. Nelson said:

> Our Father knows that when we are surrounded by uncertainty and fear, what will help us the very most is to hear his Son. I renew my plea for you to do whatever it takes to increase your spiritual capacity to receive personal revelation.[7]

The world, despite its penchant for pursuing the traditional trappings of success, has, in a way, taken on a form of biological leveling of the social playing field. The coronavirus makes no distinction between the wealthy or the poor, the popular or the obscure. Some would say this modern plague is also an opportunity for the human race to rethink a posture of humility—toward God as well as toward each other.

Current events suggest that the legacy of calamities that troubled the ancient world, however, are ripe for repeating[8] and have been foretold by almost every prophet from Moses to Paul, including (again), the ancient prophet Isaiah:

> Men shall transgress the law and break the everlasting covenant. . . . The earth also is defiled under the inhabitants thereof; because they have transgressed the laws, changed the ordinance, broken the everlasting covenant. Therefore, hath the curse devoured the earth, and they that dwell therein are desolate. . . . The city of confusion is broken down: every house is shut up, that no man may come in. . . . In the city is left desolation, and the gate is smitten with destruction. (Isaiah 24)

---

7. https://www.thechurchnews.com/leaders-and-ministry/2020-03-14/president-nelson-shares-hopeful-message-as-covid-19-outbreak-continues-177210
8. https://faithinthenews.com/5-bad-ways-history-repeated/

The tribe of man becoming humble before God is not a new concept. Since the earliest professors, priests, and prophets began to record their teachings, humanity has been admonished to remain aware of and in alignment with Divinity, as in this account from 2,500 years ago:

> If my people, which are called by my name, shall humble themselves, and pray, and seek my face, and turn from their wicked ways; then will I hear from heaven, and will forgive their sin, and will heal their land. (2 Chronicles 7)

Shortly after man was established by God in his current, intelligent form, the wheels of self-destruction quickly started turning, beginning with disobedience, followed by deception, hostility, and ultimately mortal transgression. From Adam's initial fall from grace[9] following Eve's submission to the adversary,[10] to Cain slaying his brother over a sacrificial offering and birthright,[11] to the blossoming and wilting of whole kingdoms, God has counseled His children against falling into wickedness:

> And God saw that the wickedness of man was great in the earth, and that every imagination of the thoughts of his heart was only evil continually. . . . And the Lord said, I will destroy man whom I have created from the face of the earth; both man, and beast, and the creeping thing, and the fowls of the air; for it repenteth me that I have made them. (Genesis 6)

Since the latter half of the nineteenth century, in the beginning of what has become known as America's Gilded Age[12] and loosely

---

9. http://www.dacapofoundation.com/SpecialInterest/DialTheCatholicFaith/Faith&LifeIndex/Level01-5/OKLevelOne5-06.htm
10. https://www.biblegateway.com/passage/?search=2+Corinthians+11%3A3&version=KJV
11. https://www.biblestudytools.com/bible-stories/cain-and-abel.html
12. https://www.theatlantic.com/magazine/archive/2007/06/the-dark-side-of-the-gilded-age/306012/

corresponding with the advent of the Industrial Revolution,[13] global conflict has seen a steady rise, in spite of medical setbacks along the way:

> Them that walk after the flesh in the lust of uncleanness and despise government. Presumptuous are they, self-willed, they are not afraid to speak evil of dignities. . . . But these, as natural brute beasts, made to be taken and destroyed, speak evil of the things that they understand not; and shall utterly perish in their own corruption; And shall receive the reward of unrighteousness, as they that count it pleasure to riot in the day time. (2 Peter 2)

But just as chaos and corruption have no discretion on who may be affected, a pandemic, as well, shares no logical pathway.[14] Signs of turmoil appear on a regular basis across all groups and levels of society as the world continues to embrace its own mortality, despite the trappings of political correctness. Over the last century more than 200 million people have been killed in various conflicts around the globe, largely based on the corruption of clans, despots, and rogue nations, while between 250 million and 500 million have succumbed to disease.[15]

While a medical emergency is no respecter of person, position, or place, for those who walk in faith, as admonished throughout the ages, the shadow of despair may soon fade. Consider the words spoken by leader of The Church of Jesus Christ of Latter-day Saints, President Russell M. Nelson, at an international conference on world religions in Chicago in 1993, regarding a pandemic of "spiritual drift":

> I worked as a medical doctor specializing in the teaching, research, and practice of thoracic and cardiovascular surgery. I

---

13. https://www.financierworldwide.com/crime-and-corruption-in-the-4th-industrial-revolution/#.WuvhBYgvyiM
14. https://antiguaobserver.com/no-respecter-of-persons/
15. https://ourworldindata.org/causes-of-death

> performed about seven thousand operations. During nearly four decades as a student of medical sciences, I learned to distinguish between the physical and spiritual components of the human soul. A patient could be physically weak but spiritually strong, and vice versa.
>
> . . . Duties have taken me to approximately one hundred nations of the earth, where I have observed the physical and spiritual dualism of life on a broader scale. . . . I have observed that if a great physical disaster should strike, such as a devastating earthquake or flood, people are motivated spiritually by an uncommon desire to help one another. . . . Human nature cannot be changed by reforming public policy; that kind of change comes by exposing the human mind and heart to the transforming teachings of the Lord Jesus Christ.
>
> . . . I firmly feel that the people of this world can be healed as we do our best in combatting spiritual drift—our global pandemic. Healing requires a concurrent development of the will to live, the faith to become well, and the motivation to improve our world for future generations.[16]

Political correctness and pandemic panic aside, logic, some might say, begins with the majority of the masses finding agreement regarding a common issue, rather than alienating a group for their disbelief (as we are seeing in rampant examples via the social networks).

But plagues and politics have long been intermingled in the history of times. Let's go back 700 years, when the black plague held the world in its deathly clutches. Local governments in and around Venice, primarily, as well as in other European communities, determined that the best way to address the Black Death was to improve funding for medical research and public health conditions, rather than focusing on some divine curse that befell the land. That said, however, many of the plagues and pandemics

---

16. https://abn.churchofjesuschrist.org/study/ensign/1993/11/combatting-spiritual-drift-our-global-pandemic?lang=eng&abVersion=V01&abName=GLOB88

of history have been blamed on some form of divine intervention between God's angry wrath of retribution and consequences of man's wickedness.

Martin Luther didn't agree.[17]

In 1527, the bubonic plague was making its rounds again, collecting thousands of souls along its path through the European countryside. In the eastern German hamlet of Wittenberg, the fabled German priest and icon of the Protestant Reformation stood his post and worked to treat those who were afflicted, rather than run for healthier climes:

> Those who are engaged in a spiritual ministry such as preachers and pastors must likewise remain steadfast before the peril of death. We have a plain command from Christ, "A good shepherd lays down his life for the sheep but the hireling sees the wolf coming and flees" (John 10:11). For when people are dying, they most need a spiritual ministry which strengthens and comforts their consciences by word and sacrament and in faith overcomes death. However, where enough preachers are available in one locality and they agree to encourage the other clergy to leave in order not to expose themselves needlessly to danger, I do not consider such conduct sinful because spiritual services are provided for and because they would have been ready and willing to stay if it had been necessary . . . To abandon an entire community which one has been called to govern and to leave it without official or government, exposed to all kinds of danger such as fires, murder, riots, and every imaginable disaster is a great sin . . . A man who will not help or support others unless he can do so without affecting his safety or his property will never help his neighbor. (Martin Luther [1527])[18]

A little farther east of Germany, aside from the pandemics, the politics, and power struggles, signs of civil and spiritual

---

17. https://theconversation.com/god-plagues-and-pestilence-what-history-can-teach-us-about-living-through-a-pandemic-146094
18. https://www.christianitytoday.com/ct/2020/may-web-only/martin-luther-plague-pandemic-coronavirus-covid-flee-letter.html

unrest have continued to burden the people throughout the so-called "cradle of civilization." Almost unending since the days of Israel's earliest years in captivity, those areas throughout what is now the Middle East have faced corruption and wickedness as foretold by scriptures.

> They come from a far country, from the end of heaven, even the Lord, and the weapons of his indignation, to destroy the whole land . . . and I will cause the arrogancy of the proud to cease and will lay low the haughtiness of the terrible. . . . Their children also shall be dashed to pieces before their eyes; their houses shall be spoiled, and their wives ravished. (Isaiah 13)

The foundation of all Christianity is anchored to the lands of the Mediterranean and the Middle East. Yet the very lands from which the followers of Jesus originated are seeing a dramatic decrease in its presence. As a result of the conflicts, corruption and cultural upheaval, whole Christian communities are being rounded up and summarily tortured, killed, or forced to renounce their Christian faith.[19]

As the final days of man's mortality, anarchy, wickedness, and corruption continue to approach the moral boiling point, as echoed in the words of the ancient prophet Hosea, and turning symbolic yellow flags into red ones, setting the stage for something really awful:

> There is no truth, nor mercy, nor knowledge of God in the land. By swearing, and lying, and killing, and stealing, and committing adultery, they break out, and blood toucheth blood. Therefore, shall the land mourn, and everyone that dwelleth therein shall languish. (Hosea 4)

---

19. https://cdn.americanprogress.org/wp-content/uploads/2015/03/ChristiansMiddleEast-report.pdf

Whether war or pestilence, even a historical viewpoint doesn't guarantee an easy path through life—regardless of belief or venue. Recognizing that the world continues to see many beautiful and powerful examples of fellowship, stewardship, and increased faith, despite the obstacles at times, however, might at least give us all just a bit more comfort.

Chapter Five
A Day of Darkness

"A day of darkness and of gloominess, a day of clouds and of thick darkness, as the morning spread upon the mountains: a great people and a strong; there hath not been ever the like, neither shall be any more after it, even to the years of many generations. . . . The sun shall be turned into darkness, and the moon into blood, before the great and terrible day of the Lord come."

—Joel 2

Contention has been a cancer on the history of civilization. Like threads of wool, since antiquity, the human race has found a reason to weave contention into the tapestry of our history. For some cultures—as we continue to see in the ancient regions of the world—contention has become their legacy. And somebody always loses. Fearful victims are often caught in a tug of war between the crossfire of power mongers and regional despots, with the innocent bystanders suffering as collateral damage. Meanwhile, those faithful masses are often found to ask, "Are these the days that are numbered among the stars that fall from heaven?"[1]

1. https://www.biblegateway.com/passage/?search=Revelation+9&version=KJV

During His time among the Apostles of old, Jesus was often asked about the future state of affairs, regarding His followers and Himself, their community, the world, and the fate of the human race. And throughout history, whenever conflict captures the headlines, or the human imagination as to its foretelling the end of days, Christians often turn to that passage of conversation between Jesus and His disciples:

> And as he sat upon the mount of Olives, the disciples came unto him privately, saying, Tell us, when shall these things be? and what shall be the sign of thy coming, and of the end of the world? And Jesus answered and said unto them, Take heed that no man deceive you. (Matthew 24)

But the possibility of peace in the land doesn't make good headlines. Contention, it would seem, if just good for business.[2] Sociologists suggest that it is a common trait of human nature to believe[3] the first part of something spoken as overshadowing anything else that might follow, as in the continuation of the passage in Matthew:

> And ye shall hear of wars and rumours of wars: **see that ye be not troubled: for all these things must come to pass, but the end is not yet**. For nation shall rise against nation, and kingdom against kingdom: and there shall be famines, and pestilences, and earthquakes, in divers places. (Matthew 24; emphasis added).

Jesus's message outlined in Matthew 24 has been often misunderstood as to the intent of the Lord's counsel. It has been the center of debate among biblical scholars for centuries.[4] Listing among other future events that foreshadow His return in glory, Jesus included the matter of continued conflict throughout the lands, "false Christs"

---

2. https://www.thechurchnews.com/archives/2009-07-04/if-ye-are-not-one-70778
3. https://www.lesswrong.com/posts/TiDGXt3WrQwtCdDj3/do-we-believe-everything-we-re-told
4. https://www.gotquestions.org/wars-and-rumors-of-war.html

rising up, famines, earthquakes, and what would appear to be unending persecution of his faithful followers—something that continues to happen in the very land where He walked:

> For nation shall rise against nation, and kingdom against kingdom: and there shall be earthquakes in divers places, and there shall be famines and troubles: these are the beginnings of sorrows . . . and ye shall be brought before rulers and kings for my sake, for a testimony against them . . . the brother shall betray the brother to death, and the father the son; and children shall rise up against their parents and shall cause them to be put to death. (Mark 13)

Catastrophe and perilous times seem to be on the rise[5] across the spectrum of all political and economic factions.

Just as General Sherman once quipped, "War is hell," it's also inevitable in a world full of fluctuating philosophies, inconsistent ideologies, political ambitions, and varying religious perspectives. War has shaped human evolution since the point when a brother raised a hand to kill his sibling over a birthright. Some historians have suggested modern warfare began in 1917 when President Woodrow Wilson committed ships to defend Britain's shipping lanes from ruthless German U-boats.[6]

Since World War II, almost 250 documented conflicts have been fought throughout a population of between 5 billion and 8 billion people.[7] With some statistics showing a ratio of ten non-combatant people (those who are not directly involved in a conflict)[8] being killed for every armed combatant, echoes of inspired counsel found in the book of Mark may be coming to pass:

> For in those days shall be affliction, such as was not from the beginning of the creation which God created unto this time,

---

5. http://journals.sagepub.com/doi/full/10.1177/0022343315595927
6. https://www.history.com/news/history-vault-wwi-the-first-modern-war
7. https://www.infoplease.com/history/us/major-military-operations-since-world-war-ii
8. http://washingtonsblog.com/2014/05/90-deaths-war-civilians.html

> neither shall be. . . . But in those days, after that tribulation, the sun shall be darkened, and the moon shall not give her light, and the stars of heaven shall fall, and the powers that are in heaven shall be shaken. (Mark 13)

Some critics and sociologists would suggest that humans—particularly males—are predisposed with the drive to kill other humans for the purpose of self-interest and advancement of self-promotion and prosperity.[9] In His words of caution, Jesus suggested that the specter of war will always be present, either in sight or in sound, and that the world, although remaining in a state of unrest, will not fade out of existence. At least, not yet:

> For as the lightning cometh out of the east, and shineth even unto the west; so shall also the coming of the Son of man be. . . . And then shall appear the sign of the Son of man in heaven: and then shall all the tribes of the earth mourn, and they shall see the Son of man coming in the clouds of heaven with power and great glory. (Matthew 24)

In an age when the world news is fed to every corner of the world 24/7 and ratings matter more than the truth, the speculation of war, conflict, and all-around bad news[10] does not pass without making at least a handful of headlines on a daily basis. Somewhere—usually in the Middle East and often within cannon-fire of ancient biblical sites—the world is burning. Whether Iraq or Afghanistan, Somalia or Syria, the sites of ancient battles are the sites of modern conflict:

> The burden of Damascus. Behold, Damascus is taken away from being a city, and it shall be a ruinous heap. . . . In that day shall his strong cities be as a forsaken bough, and an uppermost branch, which they left because of the children of Israel: and there shall be desolation. Because thou hast forgotten the God of thy salvation, and hast not been mindful of the rock of thy strength. (Isaiah 17)

---

9. https://www.scientificamerican.com/article/war-is-not-part-of-human-nature/
10. http://www.bbc.com/future/story/20140728-why-is-all-the-news-bad

Jesus's own half-brother, the Apostle James, in his eponymous tome, identified the origins of war as being born from within the self-turmoil surrounding human worldliness and lustful desires, rather than because of societal pressures:

> From whence come wars and fighting among you? Come they not hence, even of your lusts that war in your members. Ye lust, and have not: ye kill, and desire to have, and cannot obtain: ye fight and war, yet ye have not, because ye ask not . . . Do ye think that the scripture saith in vain, The spirit that dwelleth in us lusteth to envy? . . . Wherefore he saith, God resisteth the proud, but giveth grace unto the humble. (James 4)

Will it ever end? Not likely.

Despite the warnings by apostles, prophets, and the Savior Himself, warring factions are expected to intensify as the days between man's hubris and the advent of humility at the coming of an eternal Redeemer draw to a close.[11] But throughout the scriptures, in counsel given by Isaiah, Joel, James, Joshua, and Jesus, despite the presence of wars and rumors of wars, those who are faithful—as counseled by God's appointed stewards—may find peace amidst the storms.

The world continues to unfold in a way in which the commodity of peace seems unattainable. Armed conflict, terrorism, criminal factions, and war notwithstanding, many people in the world face conflict as a matter of daily life. Whether man-made or by natural causes, including hurricanes, tsunamis, earthquakes, or volcanoes, for example, the threat to peace in our time is as ever-present as history has always revealed it to be. In days of old, when tribes of men would hunt for their livelihood, rival tribes would fight for competing tracts of hunting ground. Dominating forces would kill their male counterparts, take their women, and kill off or (if they were lucky) assimilate any children.[12]

---

11. http://www.jewishroots.net/library/prophecy/daniel/daniel-9-24-27/war-will-continue.html
12. https://www.uky.edu/~eushe2/Pajares/moral.html

Despite the current state of affairs, hostilities, battles, and bloodshed, the hope—declared Isaiah—springs not from any power of diplomatic reasoning, but from the coming of the Redeemer Himself:

> Let us go up to the mountain of the Lord, to the house of the God of Jacob; and he will teach us of his ways, and we will walk in his paths: for out of Zion shall go forth the law, and the word of the Lord from Jerusalem . . . and they shall beat their swords into plowshares, and their spears into pruninghooks: nation shall not lift up sword against nation, neither shall they learn war any more. (Isaiah 2)

Again, according to James, it all starts with being kind to our neighbor, staying close to God's witness, following a few basic precepts of divine guidance, and living a peaceable life. And it's a definite requisite trait that mankind will learn—one way or another—before the end of our mortal probation:

> Submit yourselves therefore to God. Resist the devil, and he will flee from you. Draw nigh to God, and he will draw nigh to you. . . . Humble yourselves in the sight of the Lord, and he shall lift you up. . . . I exhort therefore, that, first of all, supplications, prayers, intercessions, and giving of thanks, be made for all men; For kings, and for all that are in authority; that we may lead a quiet and peaceable life in all godliness and honesty. (James 4)

Can man change his natural characteristics? Jesus seemed to think so.

Chapter Six
A Great Mourning

"And I will pour upon the house of David, and upon the inhabitants of Jerusalem, the spirit of grace and of supplications: and they shall look upon me whom they have pierced, and they shall mourn for him, as one mourneth for his only son, and shall be in bitterness for him, as one that is in bitterness for his firstborn. In that day shall there be a great mourning in Jerusalem."

—Zechariah 12

In a letter he wrote to the mayor and councilmen of Atlanta ahead of razing the city,[1] Union Army General William Tecumseh Sherman referred to the ravages of armed conflict and coined a phrase for the ages—one that has become the standard in describing conflict in the most profound and simplest of terms: War is hell!

But what of the "hell" that was described as that final war that would encompass all of man's struggles and conflicts and stand as the ultimate battle—that decisive catastrophic event referred to by Christians as "Armageddon?"[2] Originally a noted place in the ancient

1. http://www.rjgeib.com/thoughts/sherman/sherman-to-burn-atlanta.html
2. http://www.dictionary.com/browse/armageddon

hilltop of Megiddo, the term has become the watchword indicating the ultimate battle between good and evil.[3]

Perhaps one of the more speculated events in foretelling the Lord's return has been the matter of "wars and rumors of wars," and the fabled Battle of Armageddon, as described by the late American Reverend Billy Graham as "a war to eclipse anything the world has ever seen."[4]

While the beloved Reverend Graham recounted the book of Revelation, like many Christian scholars in anticipation of a continuation of man's penchant for self-destruction, what if the stage has already been set for the whole "Armageddon" thing?

Some scholars, eschatologists, and evangelists might agree that now is the time to consider what's inevitable. Excerpts from John's Revelation suggest that those who keep a close eye on the signs of the times may have just a bit less to worry about:

> And he gathered them together into a place called in the Hebrew tongue Armageddon. . . . And there were voices, and thunders, and lightnings; and there was a great earthquake, such as was not since men were upon the earth, so mighty an earthquake, and so great. . . . And there fell upon men a great hail out of heaven, every stone about the weight of a talent: and men blasphemed God because of the plague of the hail; for the plague thereof was exceeding great. (Revelation 16)

The word *Armageddon* originates from the composite Hebrew phrase *Har Megiddo*,[5] in reference to a battle site in ancient Mesopotamia,[6] where in a period between 1479 and 1457 BC, the Egyptian Pharaoh Thutmose III campaigned against the vassal states of Canaan, led by the king of Kadesh (ancient Syria). While there

3. https://www.merriam-webster.com/dictionary/Armageddon
4. https://billygraham.org/answer/what-is-the-battle-of-armageddon/
5. https://www.ucg.org/world-news-and-prophecy/a-place-called-megiddo-the-worlds-battleground
6. http://www.reshafim.org.il/ad/egypt/megiddobattle.htm

have been many battles fought on the plains of Megiddo,[7] this "great war" of its time lasted seven months and was the first of many conflicts fought on the plains of Megiddo (although the term *Armageddon* never appears in the Old Testament).

But history (and religious doctrine of many Christian sects) is replete with references to "great wars." The American Civil War, as an example, was often referred to as the "Great War between the North and South," with more than 620,000 soldiers being killed in that war alone.[8] World War I has historically been referred to as the "Great War" and saw an eight-year global conflict involving thirty-two countries and the loss of nearly 40 million souls. Anyone who was around for World War II would testify of the profound impact it had on the human race, with a global death toll exceeding 80 million!

What, then, of this "Armageddon" referenced by John in Revelation 16:16?

> And he gathered them together into a place called in the Hebrew tongue Armageddon. (Revelation 16:16)

And how does John's reference to this great battle correlate with the Lord's return, as many Christian leaders[9] from the past two millennia have foretold?

According to accounts in the books of Joel and Isaiah in the Old Testament and Revelation in the New Testament, the last great war of mankind is to take place between two massive armies. The battle includes the armies of Gog and Magog, from countries north of Israel.

This final battle, according to Christian tradition, marks the beginning of the end of world conflict.[10] Events preceding the battle of Armageddon are forecast to resemble much of what we are currently

7. https://www.worldhistory.org/article/1101/thutmose-iii-at-the-battle-of-megiddo/
8. https://ehistory.osu.edu/exhibitions/cwsurgeon/cwsurgeon/statistics
9. https://bible.org/seriespage/13-armageddon-and-second-coming-christ
10. https://www.haaretz.com/israel-news/.premium.MAGAZINE-armageddon-101-the-true-history-of-the-end-of-the-world-1.6079081

seeing running rampant throughout the Middle East. Prophecies of nations collapsing and evil sinking to new levels of malevolence seem to be part of the formula for man's appetite for destruction and serve as the impetus for the end of days.

Modern-day philosophies and interpretation of John's Revelation suggest that upon the arrival of the risen Messiah, the world will be returned to a state of glorified existence, similar to that in which it was found in the Garden of Eden. This transformation will be necessary to provide safe harbor for those eternal beings (the righteous souls who walked the earth throughout time) who will eventually visit and ultimately inhabit the earth.

But all hell has to break loose first.

Many of the Old Testament prophets, including Isaiah, Jeremiah, Ezekiel, Daniel, and Zechariah, referenced some form of final ultimate conflict between global forces in an all-in battle for the liberty of the human race:

> Howl ye; for the day of the Lord is at hand; it shall come as a destruction from the Almighty. Therefore, shall all hands be faint, and every man's heart shall melt: And they shall be afraid: pangs and sorrows shall take hold of them; they shall be in pain as a woman that travaileth: they shall be amazed one at another; their faces shall be as flames. Behold, the day of the Lord cometh, cruel both with wrath and fierce anger, to lay the land desolate: and he shall destroy the sinners thereof out of it. For the stars of heaven and the constellations thereof shall not give their light: the sun shall be darkened in his going forth, and the moon shall not cause her light to shine. And I will punish the world for their evil, and the wicked for their iniquity; and I will cause the arrogancy of the proud to cease and will lay low the haughtiness of the terrible. (Isaiah 13)

Some biblical scholars suggest Isaiah's reference to "the Day of the Lord" being at hand refers to parallel historical events: one referring to a battle in which Babylon (Hebrew captors during Isaiah's time) would fall desolate (which what is now present-day Iraq since has) and to a modern-day "Babylon," which will yet fall.

Babylon, in ancient times, was the greatest power in the land and soon became the symbol in language to represent powerful nations that ruled with impunity, as was referred to by John in his Revelation:

> I saw another angel come down from heaven, having great power; and the earth was lightened with his glory. And he cried mightily with a strong voice, saying, Babylon the great is fallen, is fallen, and is become the habitation of devils, and the hold of every foul spirit, and a cage of every unclean and hateful bird. For all nations have drunk of the wine of the wrath of her fornication, and the kings of the earth have committed fornication with her, and the merchants of the earth are waxed rich through the abundance of her delicacies. (Revelation 18)

While historians suggest much of Revelation pertains to John's lightly veiled and often encoded grievances toward the empire of Rome[11] (and the ultimate redemption to be provided by the Savior upon his return), scholars suggest John is also implying the destruction of a great and powerful (and wicked) nation that has come to find itself at-odds with God.

The gears, according to some of the signs foretold by Ezekiel and Zechariah, have already been set in motion regarding the disposition of Israel:

- It will be gathered (Ezekiel 36). The modern nation of Israel was made official in 1948.
- Jerusalem will stand as the capital of the Jewish people worldwide (Zechariah 1–2). Jerusalem is the recognized capital of the Jewish state, and at present, even the United States relocated its embassy from Tel Aviv to Jerusalem in recognition of this fact.
- It will become "as a mighty men, [who] will tread down their enemies" (Zechariah 10:5). The nation-state of Israel is a nuclear power and is respected as a central force of liberty

---

11. https://hermeneutics.stackexchange.com/questions/9052/was-the-revelation-written-in-code-to-hide-it-from-the-romans

and independence throughout the Middle East and the world (and amidst current chaos between Syria, Iraq, Palestine, and its surrounding adversaries, Israel remains a tenuous territory of controversy and border conflict).

But who are these characters, Gog and Magog?

Although the name Gog of Ezekiel's time suggests no particular individual, Ezekiel (and later in John's Revelation) suggests that Gog and his land, represented by Magog, symbolize the great Babylonian heretics who would stand against Israel, God, and all that is part of God's plan. While Jewish eschatology[12] looks to the battle of Gog and Magog as the point where their promised Messiah will finally arrive on the scene and redeem them from their oppressors, Christians look at the battle of Armageddon as man's final conflict before God calls an end to all of the mayhem.

> For the king of the north shall return, and shall set forth a multitude greater than the former, and shall certainly come after certain years with a great army and with much riches . . . also the robbers of thy people shall exalt themselves to establish the vision; but they shall fall. . . . So the king of the north shall come, and cast up a mount, and take the most fenced cities: and the arms of the south shall not withstand, neither his chosen people, neither shall there be any strength to withstand. (Daniel 11)

Daniel's prophecy of the coming of a "king of the north" with a "great army" [13] to conquer the land has been interpreted to be anyone from Alexander the Great to a yet-to-be identified force.

The prophecies of the Old and New Testaments, as well as current signs of the times, suggest that despite whatever forces that may be present, which will bring upon Israel what are foretold to be its darkest days yet, there's going to be hell to pay for Gog, Magog, and everyone else who stands between Christ and His people.

---

12. http://www.jewishencyclopedia.com/articles/5849-eschatology
13. Daniel 11

With more than 4,000 years of conflict surrounding a small area some sixty miles outside of Jerusalem, where generations of Jews, Gentiles, Muslims, and Mesopotamians have laid each other to waste, a common theme would suggest that everybody has it in for Israel—whether symbolic or literally—and the battle with Gog and Magog, as described by the Old Testament prophet Ezekiel, and later by John, will begin (and end) with one final siege of Jerusalem. But unlike the time of the Crusades, when Christian kings sought to liberate the Holy Land from its heathen hosts, the battle for Israel will, according to the prophets of old (and a few modern ones), be for the final redemption of the human race.

PART THREE
THE ARROGANCE OF THE PROUD

"Each generation imagines itself to be more intelligent than the one that went before it, and wiser than the one that comes after it."

—George Orwell, Collected Essays[1]

Christianity teaches that there will be a reckoning of souls upon the closing days of man on the earth, meaning that the righteous will be united with Jesus at His coming, being spared God's angry wrath upon a prideful, arrogant world, while there will be "hell to pay" for those who have chosen wickedness as a way of life.[2] Although many cultures throughout history claimed to know when the Lord will return, the scriptures record that even Christ Himself does not know the day God will send Him back to us.

Now, almost 2,000 years since Jesus's departure, the Christian world still looks to the day when Jesus will return. We live in a time when the men Paul wrote of seem to walk among us en masse:

1. https://orwelllibrary.files.wordpress.com/2014/08/orwell-george-collected-essays-journalism-letters-vol-4-1945-1950-secker-warburg-19681.pdf
2. https://www.openbible.info/topics/in_the_last_days

> Men shall be lovers of their own selves, covetous, boasters, proud, blasphemers, disobedient to parents, unthankful, unholy, without natural affection, trucebreakers, false accusers, incontinent, fierce, despisers of those that are good, traitors, heady, high-minded, lovers of pleasures more than lovers of God; having a form of godliness but denying the power thereof: from such turn away. (2 Timothy 3)

After the conditions of captivity and the remorse that accompanies it, as mentioned as part of a somewhat modified pride cycle, in part three, let's examine the history and social evolution of Christian religious pride and arrogance throughout the post-apostolic period, and how such hubris held back the ability to recover (and when humility won the day, the difference it made).

By no means is this designed to be a definitive treatise on Christian or Jewish hubris. A study on the indicators of the world as it journeys through the pride cycle (and leading up to what modern-day religious prophets and apostles would say is the last dispensation), however, must consider the timeline and intersections between Jews and Gentiles, as foreseen by the ancient prophets. . . .

* * *

. . . The storm of iniquity, some Christian scholars suggest,[3] is boiling on the horizon.

Matters of virtue, self-control, traditional marriage, and the pursuit of what some Christian scholars believe to be a wanton abandonment of all righteousness are being replaced with a sort-of anything goes way of life. In the Old Testament, the standard for bad living was measured in Sodom and Gomorrah:

> And when the morning arose, then the angels hastened Lot, saying, Arise, take thy wife, and thy two daughters, which are here; lest thou be consumed in the iniquity of the city. . . . And it came to pass, when they had brought them forth abroad, that he said,

3. http://www.biblesabbath.org/bacchiocchi/endtimewickedness.html

> Escape for thy life; look not behind thee, neither stay thou in all the plain; escape to the mountain, lest thou be consumed. (Genesis 19)

Faithful disciples of Christ infer the modern rise in arrogance and wickedness as sign of stronger adversarial forces that tug on the delicate fabric of righteousness, signaling the dusk of the human race.[4] Their position that Satan's success has grown exponentially as being linked to the improvement of mass-communications, is largely founded upon the notion that modern technology brings increased corruption[5] in its shadow:

> All of our exalted technological progress, civilization for that matter, is comparable to an axe in the hand of a pathological criminal. (Albert Einstein [1917])[6]

In a letter written to his friend Heinrich Zangger in 1917, noted physicist Albert Einstein was concerned about the advances of science that he saw being fueled by the work done behind the scenes during World War I and the potential misuse of advances in science by arrogant power-mongers of his time. His letter about the morality of arrogance outweighing charity continued:

> How is it at all possible that this culture-loving era could be so monstrously amoral? More and more I come to value charity and love of one's fellow being above everything else. (Albert Einstein [1917])

Christians have long argued that Satan works to gain access and manipulate our thoughts and emotional responses by "helping" improve our access to anything that can be maligned or exploited for

4. https://www.christianpost.com/news/4-reasons-many-christians-believe-the-end-times-are-near-164280/
5. https://www.theatlantic.com/science/archive/2016/03/corruption-honesty/472779/
6. https://einsteinpapers.press.princeton.edu/vol10-trans/76

his purposes.[7] Multi-sensory programs and images, popular recordings that even many contemporary artists would argue against describing as "music," as well as the excessive stimulus of physical senses, have all become common fare of adversarial trappings in the digital age.

The current affairs of a world in turmoil includes a transition to a more humanistic society in which modesty and conservative viewpoints on God appear to be becoming out-of-fashion with the rise in self-identity, gender neutrality, and political correctness.

Ancient text would surmise that we haven't learned to advance out of this cycle, as recorded in these passages more than 2,500 years ago:

> Let not arrogancy come out of your mouth: for the Lord is a God of knowledge, and by him actions are weighed. . . . And I will punish the world for their evil, and the wicked for their iniquity; and I will cause the arrogancy of the proud to cease and will lay low the haughtiness of the terrible. (1 Samuel 2; Isaiah 13)

Apostasy is the word used to describe the abandoning or denouncement of divine authority, or trading the desire to follow God for the arrogance of self-interest.

A surefire sign of the last days, say many eschatologists, is the increased focus on matters concerning self-love, the bending of traditional values for the sake of new social norms, and an increased focus on matters of little or no long-term value. First-century Rome, according to Paul in his letter to his traveling companion, Timothy, had some of the similar problems we are seeing today:

> For men shall be lovers of their own selves, covetous, boasters, proud, blasphemers, disobedient to parents, unthankful, unholy, Without natural affection, trucebreakers, false accusers, incontinent, fierce, despisers of those that are good, Traitors, heady, highminded, lovers of pleasures more than lovers of God; Having a form of godliness but denying the power thereof: from such turn away. (2 Timothy 3)

---

7. https://www.littlelightstudios.tv/knowledge-shall-increased-shall-satans-deceptions/

Although many people may be unfamiliar with the concept of an apostasy, the cycle of civilizations that have renounced their faith in God has a seen recurring pattern in the cycle of social pride throughout history, and some reports indicate an increase in a breach between the once-faithful and the newfound cynic.[8] During the time referred to as the antediluvian period, or prior to the Great Flood,[9] the people of Noah's age had abandoned the laws that were established for them by God, and as a consequence, they were wiped from the earth. Throughout the many generations since, there have been periods of apostasy in the world in which God's divine direction ceased to be permitted in man's behalf, and darkness would fall across the land:

> And as it was in the days of Noe, so shall it be also in the days of the Son of man. . . . Likewise also as it was in the days of Lot. . . . And because iniquity shall abound, the love of many shall wax cold. . . . For then shall be great tribulation, such as was not since the beginning of the world to this time, no, nor ever shall be. (Luke 17; Matthew 24)

Christians assume Jesus referenced the times of Noah and Lot, not because of their conducting their day-to-day lives, but because of their abandonment of things holy for things worldly. Further, the Lord suggests that the world will "wax cold" similar to those times again, as an indication to foreshadow his triumphant return:

> And then shall appear the sign of the Son of man in heaven: and then shall all the tribes of the earth mourn, and they shall see the Son of man coming in the clouds of heaven with power and great glory. (Matthew 24)

Many religious scholars agree that a Great Apostasy[10] or falling away from faith took place following the death of the last of the apostles of Christ's era. By the end of the first century AD the rightful order

---

8. https://billygraham.org/answer/why-are-people-losing-faith-in-god/
9. https://www.earthhistory.org.uk/before-the-cataclysm/before-the-flood
10. https://www.gotquestions.org/great-apostasy.html

and sacred ordinances established by Christ through His ordained apostles vanished from the world. Without the sanctioned governance of an anointed body of leadership, religious historians suggest the people were left to their own understandings as to what and who to trust, regarding the word and will of the Almighty, as anticipated by the Apostle Paul to the faithful of Rome:

> And even as they did not like to retain God in their knowledge, God gave them over to a reprobate mind, to do those things which are not convenient; Being filled with all unrighteousness, fornication, wickedness, covetousness, maliciousness; full of envy, murder, debate, deceit, malignity; whisperers, Backbiters, haters of God. (Romans 1)

Again, turning to Paul, like his predecessor from an earlier period in history, Paul often counseled as Isaiah did, regarding the future state of civilization in which godlessness prevailed:

> Ah sinful nation, a people laden with iniquity, a seed of evildoers, children that are corrupters: they have forsaken the Lord, they have provoked the Holy One of Israel unto anger, they are gone away backward . . . evil men and seducers shall wax worse and worse, deceiving, and being deceived. (Isaiah 1; 2 Timothy 3)

To Jesus's admonition to His Apostles as recorded in Matthew, the world has seen a significant increase in wickedness, as was foretold by the ancient writer of Psalms:

> The transgression of the wicked saith within my heart, that there is no fear of God before his eyes. For he flattereth himself in his own eyes, until his iniquity be found to be hateful. The words of his mouth are iniquity and deceit: he hath left off to be wise, and to do good. He deviseth mischief upon his bed; he setteth himself in a way that is not good; he abhorreth not evil. (Psalm 36)

One common theme in the growing ranks of the desensitized humanistic ideology,[11] Christians argue, is the belief that accountability should not have to yield to self-gratification, self-interest, or self-preservation, and that the human race can be "good without God."[12]

Then came the Great Awakening of 1730, which saw the rapid spread of evangelical Christianity reshape the nature of colonial ideology toward independence and away from their British overseers. Following the Boston Massacre in 1770, when British soldiers shot into a mob of angry citizens, killing five of the assembled rioters, the colonists soon formed their own loosely held government of colonial representation as part of their growing disdain for the way in which the Crown had treated the rights of the American colonists.

Given the movement toward a more "socially informed" society—one that tends to turn away from a faith-based ideal—religious scholars might ask the question, as the ancient children of Israel learned, can any of us really afford to live without God?

---

11. https://www.allaboutworldview.org/humanist-sociology-and-traditional-marriage-faq.htm
12. https://www.reasonablefaith.org/writings/popular-writings/existence-nature-of-god/can-we-be-good-without-god/

Chapter Seven
Blood and Fire

"I will pour out my spirit upon all flesh; and your sons and your daughters shall prophesy, your old men shall dream dreams, your young men shall see visions: And also upon the servants and upon the handmaids in those days will I pour out my spirit. And I will shew wonders in the heavens and in the earth, blood, and fire, and pillars of smoke. The sun shall be turned into darkness, and the moon into blood, before the great and the terrible day of the Lord come."

—Joel 2

For some people, the word *rapture* can conjure up ideas ranging from people vanishing in the streets in the blink of an eye (Thanos not included), to legions of angels marching out of the clouds behind four horse riders.

Many Christian faiths teach of a "rapture" (a word invented by British evangelist John Nelson Darby, the so-called "father of dispensationalism"),[1] and is based on an interpretation of

1. http://www.christianitytoday.com/history/people/pastorsandpreachers/john-nelson-darby.html

1 Thessalonians about the righteous followers of Jesus being "carried away in the clouds,"[2] in which those people who accepted Christ as their Savior will immediately vanish from the world when He returns. While some Christian believers teach of a time when the righteous will be called up to meet Jesus before He cleanses the world with fire, as a rule, other Christian sects take attention-to-detail one step further where Christianity leaves off: There's more to getting that spiritual ticket to ride with Christ than just admitting that He's the Messiah (and it's highly unlikely there will be any trip up into the clouds as it's often interpreted to mean).

By contrast, the Millennium is the period of time that members of The Church of Jesus Christ of Latter-day Saints say represents the 1,000 years following the return of Christ and is frequently a general reference point as being the final period before the last judgment. As foretold by the prophets of old, the Millennium will be heralded by earthquakes, giant storms, fire in the sky, and wars and rumors of wars, as those who remain caught in the cycle of pride continue to ignore the reality of their fate:

> This know also, that in the last days perilous times shall come. For men shall be lovers of their own selves, covetous, boasters, proud, blasphemers, disobedient to parents, unthankful, unholy, Without natural affection, trucebreakers, false accusers, incontinent, fierce, despisers of those that are good, Traitors, heady, high-minded, lovers of pleasures more than lovers of God; Having a form of godliness but denying the power thereof: from such turn away. (2 Timothy)

For more than 2,000 years, legend, prophecies, oracles, and even astronomers have deliberated on the impression that the clock is winding down on mortality. Ask ten different people from ten different Christian faiths, and chances are, there will be ten different perspectives all rooted in some sense of "doctrine" as to the coming of "That Great and Dreadful Day"—the Second Coming of Christ. Books have been written, movies produced, even songs sung about the

---

2. https://bible.org/question/where-did-term-8216rapture%E2%80%99-come

Millennium.[3] And there has been plenty of wailing and gnashing of teeth over false alarms throughout history. From a pure sense of biblical scholarship, as recorded by John in Revelation 20, the Millennium describes that period when Satan is bound during the 1,000-year ministry of the resurrected Christ[4] on earth.

Everybody seems to have an insider track on the ultimate Christian events corresponding with the Second Coming of Christ. Just after AD 1000, the long-standing myth popularized by inaccurate accounts suggested that religious radicals throughout Medieval Europe were so convinced that the End of Days was upon them that some of the more zealous of the followers flung themselves from mountaintops, thinking their offering would be sufficient compensation for their misdeeds in life.[5] While some records report of some Christian extremists walled themselves into caves, even stopped talking and eating for as long as they could before succumbing to fatigue, insanity, or death, many Christians surrendered their earthly belongings to the Church, anticipating that their penance (and meager offerings) would benefit them upon the Lord's return. Given the lack of education about the actual date and time from day to day, most faithful followers had no idea what day or year it was and remained unaffected at the passing of the first millennium. Conversely, however, as time passed (and the resurrected Jesus was nowhere to be found), the Church offered no refunds on those possessions given.[6]

Speaking of "blood and fire," the so-called last days were prophesied of many hundreds of years before the first millennium. Around the year 750 BC, back when King Uzziah was leading the Kingdom of Judah to more than fifty years of innovation and political advancement, the prophet Amos wrote of the significance of the bond between man, earth, and heaven, in a bit of foreshadowing of the things that would soon follow:

---

3. https://www.ligonier.org/learn/series/last_days_according_to_jesus/the-millennium-938/
4. https://www.biblegateway.com/passage/?search=Revelation+20&version=NKJV
5. https://www.smithsonianmag.com/history/terror-in-ad-1000-55965537/
6. https://www.nytimes.com/1999/07/17/nyregion/beliefs-millennial-fears-year-1000-apocalypse-then-apocalypse-now-apocalypse.html

> The words of Amos, who was among the herdmen of Tekoa, which he saw concerning Israel in the days of Uzziah king of Judah, and in the days of Jeroboam the son of Joash king of Israel, two years before the earthquake. And he said, The Lord will roar from Zion, and utter his voice from Jerusalem; and the habitations of the shepherds shall mourn, and the top of Carmel shall wither. (Amos 1)

Whether Amos was referring to Uzziah's unrighteous behavior in entering the temple without authorization as the motivation for the 8+ magnitude earthquake that impacted ancient Israel in ~750 BC is left to the ages. If the oracles of legend and the prophets of old (as well as a few of the newer ones from our own day) are to be believed, one common thread that appears as a constant reminder is that the events of nature often coincide with the actions of a grieving God, a wicked culture, and a restless world.[7]

One thing is certain: the fact that Amos delivered his speech a full two years before the earthquake leveled most of Judah, leaving the Hebrew culture in a bit of a shock. The idea of altars cracking (Amos 3:14), houses being destroyed (Amos 6:10–11), and the earth itself trembling (Amos 8:8) didn't seem so far removed two years after the shepherd-farmer made his declaration, as all of Judah was sweeping up the rubble.

Fast-forward two centuries and the apocalyptic tone of Joel suggests the downfall, not just of the land on which the Hebrew kingdom stands—but the very kingdom of Jerusalem itself:

> Blow ye the trumpet in Zion, and sound an alarm in my holy mountain: let all the inhabitants of the land tremble: for the day of the Lord cometh, for it is nigh at hand; A day of darkness and of gloominess, a day of clouds and of thick darkness, as the morning spread upon the mountains: a great people and a strong; there hath

7. https://abn.churchofjesuschrist.org/study/general-conference/2004/04/preparation-for-the-second-coming?lang=eng&abVersion=V01&abName=GLOB88

> not been ever the like, neither shall be any more after it, even to the years of many generations. (Joel 2)

In theory, if you were a Hebrew during Joel's time, life was a lot less complicated. As a people, you'd head into town once a year, go to the temple and give thanks for your crops and livestock, live the law of Moses, raise your family, and stay close to the word of God as it was prescribed by the tribal leaders.

In theory.

By consequence, however, Joel, like the prophets before him and those who would follow, saw the destruction of his people—not because of the conquest by another nation (although that didn't help matters) but because of their consistent desire to step out of line with the Powers-that-Be (God), resulting in destruction, captivity, and generations of despair. The shift in control for both the upper and lower kingdoms remained in a constant state of turmoil, and Christian scholars have suggested this similarity can be seen today, as people choose to abandon godly principles for worldly trappings (another sign of the last dispensation):

> And now come I to thee; and these things I speak in the world, that they might have my joy fulfilled in themselves. I have given them thy word; and the world hath hated them, because they are not of the world, even as I am not of the world. I pray not that thou shouldest take them out of the world, but that thou shouldest keep them from the evil. They are not of the world, even as I am not of the world. Sanctify them through thy truth: thy word is truth. As thou hast sent me into the world, even so have I also sent them into the world. And for their sakes I sanctify myself, that they also might be sanctified through the truth. (John 17:13–19)

Many religious scholars question the so-called "Israelization" of certain Christian groups because of their close association and desire to be aligned with Israel, which is considered to be the original Church of God.[8]

Whether out of necessity or by prophecy, the gathering of Israel has already begun. On May 14, 1948, the nation of Israel was restored to a portion of its original land and has continued to make efforts to extend its locus of influence in the region and throughout the world. Then there's the one-two punch offered by Joel and Luke, respectively:

> And I will shew wonders in the heavens and in the earth, blood, and fire, and pillars of smoke. The sun shall be turned into darkness, and the moon into blood, before the great and terrible day of the Lord come. (Joel 2:30-31)

> And I will shew wonders in heaven above, and signs in the earth beneath; blood, and fire, and vapour of smoke. (Acts 2:19)

Some scholars would suggest Joel's prophecy began to be fulfilled on the Day of Pentecost, when the Holy Ghost was left in the world upon the Lord's final ascension to heaven. Others would suggest that "blood and fire" is a reference to the vengeance the Lord will impose upon those who betrayed Him upon His final return, in alignment with the activities in ancient Egypt surrounding Passover.

In some of the more modern corners of Christianity, such as the doctrine of The Church of Jesus Christ of Latter-day Saints, after the return of Jesus, the world will be transformed into a glorified state.[9] This state of existence, they suggest, is the same condition the world was in when God walked with Adam and Eve in the Garden of Eden. Before the final events leading to the sunset of mortality as we know it, several pre-apocryphal events need to take place, as explained by biblical prophets, including a reunion between the nation of Israel, including all of the tribes, as described in the books of Isaiah and Jeremiah:

---

8. https://thejerusalemfund.org/2018/05/what-jerusalem-means-to-us-christian-perspectives-and-reflections-2/
9. https://abn.churchofjesuschrist.org/study/manual/teachings-joseph-smith/chapter-21?lang=eng&abVersion=V01&abName=GLOB88

> For a small moment have I forsaken thee [Israel]; but with great mercies will I gather thee. (Isaiah) 54:7)

> The children of Israel shall come, they and the children of Judah together. They shall ask the way to Zion with their faces thitherward, saying, Come, and let us join ourselves to the Lord. (Jeremiah 50)

Jeremiah also implies throughout his book of blending Jewish doctrine with the fulfillment of the law of Moses through the life and Atonement of Jesus, as He taught during His earthly ministry.

Regardless of whether it was Joel or Amos, Isaiah or Jeremiah or John, with volcanoes darkening a third of modern Europe (and forcing aircraft to be rerouted for days at a time), as was the case in with the eruption of Iceland's Eyjafjallajökull volcano in 2010,[10] or back-to-back category 5 hurricanes in the Atlantic, massive earthquakes in Mexico, and wars in the streets and fields—one might wonder whether Isaiah's words regarding God forsaking His children hasn't been extended to all of us who are watching these prophecies unfold today.

Although it might seem like we're living in a world similar to what has been prophesied, according to the prophecies, this is a picnic to what's coming.

10. https://www.icelandtravel.is/attractions/eyjafjallajokull/

CHAPTER EIGHT
THE DAY THAT COMETH

"And the day that cometh shall burn them up, saith the Lord of hosts, that it shall leave them neither root nor branch. But unto you that fear my name shall the Sun of righteousness arise with healing in his wings. . . . Behold, I will send you Elijah the prophet before the coming of the great and dreadful day of the Lord. And he shall turn the heart of the fathers to the children, and the heart of the children to their fathers."

—Malachi 4

"The end of the prophets." With those five words, the Old Testament comes to a close. Whether a declaration of Malachi's prophecy regarding the earth being consumed by fire in the last days, or just a passing remark by those biblical councils who assembled the version of what has stood as the most widely distributed book of all time, Christian eschatology supposes that in the final days of man, those who would not "remember the Law of Moses[1]" or would not turn the children's hearts to their fathers would be smitten with a curse.[2]

1. http://www.thirdelijahmessage.info/MosesLaw.html
2. https://www.biblestudytools.com/malachi/4-6-compare.html

Concern over what the world would be cursed with became a topic of great interest (and still is for many—given the current conditions of our pandemic-infused confusion):

> Even from the days of your fathers ye are gone away from mine ordinances and have not kept them. Return unto me, and I will return unto you, saith the Lord of hosts. . . . Then shall ye return, and discern between the righteous and the wicked, between him that serveth God and him that serveth him not. . . . And he shall turn the heart of the fathers to the children, and the heart of the children to their fathers, lest I come and smite the earth with a curse. (Malachi 3–4)

Malachi's prophecies foretell of the coming consequences of a prideful and wicked world, and more than 2,000 years ago, the Jews thought Malachi's prophecies were coming to pass, as a man with the "spirit of Elijah" came forth out of the wilderness. Scholars and many theologians suggest this prophecy was partially fulfilled[3] with John the Baptist, and when Jesus Himself was asked about the foretelling, He referred to his cousin, John, as fulfillment of that prophecy, as He explained in the account by Matthew.[4]

But what of the whole "fire and brimstone" that was foreshadowed?

The Roman empire wasn't the best place to practice Christianity during the first and second centuries. After the mass slaughter of the general Christian population by Nero during the mid-70s, the disciples of Jesus went underground, forming house churches, with competing philosophies emerging almost immediately.

A community within an empire that would follow someone other than a divinely appointed ruler did not sit well in the courts of Rome.[5] It was one thing to manage the traditional Jewish subculture, who had been complaining about their oppression for generations. But it was another to consider that a wandering man from the deserts of Galilee

---

3. https://doctrine.org/john-the-baptist-as-elijah
4. https://www.biblegateway.com/passage/?search=Matthew+11&version=KJV
5. http://www.christianitytoday.com/history/issues/issue-27/persecution-in-early-church-did-you-know.html

and a handful of his followers could sway even the Jews to rethink their religious position. And thus, the Christian persecution began. Both Jew and Gentile began to follow the words of Jesus, as taught by His appointed apostles, which resulted in tremendous losses, tragedy, and almost the total extinction of an entire culture.

The ancient church of Christ was established based on a hierarchal structure[6] and included various roles, including evangelists, ministers, and other religious leaders who were called into specific positions for the administration of the Church. The organization and structure of the Church continued under the anointing of Peter, who was given the keys of authority by Jesus, prior to Christ's ascension. Peter held those keys until his death in Rome in AD 66. Subsequent Apostles, including Andronicus, Stephen, Barnabas, and even the great Apostle Paul, served as special witnesses of Christ's teaching, under the direction of Peter.

James, the brother of Christ, for example, although not one of the original Twelve Apostles, was called to the apostleship after the resurrection and eventually served as a bishop in Jerusalem (chosen and anointed by Peter), according to the first-century writings of Clement of Rome:

> To James, the lord, and the bishop of bishops, who rules Jerusalem, the holy church of the Hebrews, and the churches everywhere excellently rounded by the providence of God, with the elders and deacons, and the rest of the brethren, peace be always. (Epistle of Clement)[7]

By way of odd coincidence, there were at least three major references to different men named James in the New Testament: "James the Just," who was the brother of Jesus,[8] wrote the Epistle of James in the New Testament; James, the son of Zebedee, who was one of

---

6. http://factsanddetails.com/world/cat55/sub353/item1405.html
7. https://www.biblestudytools.com/history/early-church-fathers/ante-nicene/vol-8-third-fourth-centuries/pseudo-clementine-literature/epistle-of-clement-to-james.html
8. http://www.churchhistory101.com/century1-p6.php

the Lord's closest personal assistants (along with the other son of Zebedee—John—and Peter); and James, the son of Alphaeus, who was also one of Jesus's original Twelve.

Like most Christians of antiquity, the Christians throughout the empire did not congregate into single groups but would choose instead to meet in house churches and study the word of the Lord, as referenced by Paul in his letter to members of the church in Rome:

> Greet Priscilla and Aquila my helpers in Christ Jesus . . . unto whom not only I give thanks, but also all the churches of the Gentiles. . . . Likewise greet the church that is in their house. Salute my well-beloved Epænetus, who is the firstfruits of Achaia unto Christ. (Romans 16)

Subsequently, scores of thousands of people, mostly Christian factionalists, were slaughtered at the games in the Flavian Amphitheater, more commonly known as the Colosseum. The Colosseum was commissioned by the emperor Vespasian in AD 69 and was later completed by his son Titus. According to historical records, during its first full year of operation, an average of one person was killed every five minutes around the clock as part of the Roman's pagan and often carnal festivities, usually from mock battles and executions.[9] The killings spanned nearly 400 years, with an estimated 400,000 people and more than one million animals being slaughtered for entertainment.

Knowing that being subject to higher laws was inevitable, Paul wrote of governance to the Christians of ancient Rome:

> Let every soul be subject unto the higher powers. For there is no power but of God: the powers that be are ordained of God. . . . For rulers are not a terror to good works, but to the evil. Wilt thou then not be afraid of the power? do that which is good, and thou shalt have praise of the same: For he is the minister of God to thee for good. But if thou do that which is evil, be afraid; for he beareth not the sword in vain: for he is the minister of God. (Romans 13)

---

9. http://www.the-colosseum.net/history/martyrium_en.htm

With the last apostles rounded up and executed, however, the church no longer had direct leadership, and a whole new wave of people rose up to become self-appointed leaders. Consequently, religious chapters that were organized by the likes of Stephen, James, Timothy, and Paul were left to their own designs and influences of the local cultures. Under the reign of Roman Caesars, the empire took less than a century to finally destroy God's anointed leaders.

By the beginning of the fourth century, Rome was so large it was the edict of the emperor Diocletian that four lesser kings (two Augustuses and two Caesars) assisted in leadership to fend off the barbarian enemies from the north (the Goths, Vandals, and so on). The tetrarchy, as it was known,[10] was not very successful, and within a few years, everybody wanted the throne for themselves.

Prior to its overthrow by the Goths in the fifth century, Rome's borders covered almost all of the Mediterranean, from the shores of the Caspian Sea in the east, to Brittania in the northwest, and Egypt in the south. Maintaining not only an empire but also such a vast cross-cultural community grew more challenging for the senate and for Caesar, and the last thing on their minds was the idea that a new faith would rise up and topple the old gods.

The church of God, as it was organized by Christ and further established by the Apostles throughout the lands, was gone from its original state, and so was its authority. Over the course of the next three centuries, religious factionalism began to creep into the Roman government, and secularism infiltrated the pure church of God, while the empire outgrew itself, requiring not one but four leaders.

One of the four rulers of the time, Constantine,[11] was the son of a Roman senator and a Christian-convert wife. Constantine became a powerful military leader and eventually rose to become Caesar of the Western Empire. By the fourth century, the whispers of the Good Shepherd and His Apostles had grown into a shout across the empire. Adding ambivalence to insult, Christian factions were rising in numbers and threatened to kick even Jupiter himself—the supreme deity

---

10. https://courses.lumenlearning.com/suny-hccc-worldhistory/chapter/diocletian-and-the-tetrarchy/
11. http://www.christianitytoday.com/history/people/rulers/constantine.html

of the ancient Romans—off of his throne and shake the empire to its core, which it did in 313 when the new emperor Constantine authored an imperial edict that protected the rights of the growing population of Christian worship throughout the empire.

By the beginning of the fourth century, the conquests of Constantine resulted in reunifying Rome under one leader.[12] Perhaps out of hubris or in some twist of divine inspiration, the Roman regent decided to move the ancient capital of the empire from Rome to the ancient port town of Byzantium on the Black Sea. Historically recognized as the crossroads between Eastern Europe and everything else, moving the capital city to the newly named Constantinople planted the seeds of the destruction of the secular empire of the day, to be replaced by what became a religious empire throughout the world by the close of the first millennium.

Constantine's changing the central capital of the empire from Rome to what is now Istanbul had a significant impact on the religion of the day. It created a religious center in the eastern portion of the region, which was highly influenced by Greek tradition, while the city of Rome was left to the devices of local Christian leaders, who claimed to be the official headquarters of the legacy church of Christ.

Looking ahead 600 years, long after the battle between Leo and John[13] (the respective bishops of Rome and Constantinople in 588), to 1074, the Roman Catholic Church was fully established as the religious backbone throughout Europe and the known world. In an ironic twist of direction, religious domination was again in full swing in Eastern Europe and the Middle East, but this time, without any formal spiritual leadership sanctioned by God. Under the direction of Pope Gregory and the Roman Catholic Church, the first Crusades began, with a focus on ridding the Holy Land of the many religious "infidels" who inhabited it—namely, those who were not Christian (or Catholic). The cycle of conquest, political will, and large-scale

---

12. http://www.thenagain.info/WebChron/EastEurope/ConstantineConverts.html
13. https://www.revolvy.com/main/index.php?s=Siege%20of%20Dorostolon&item_type=topic

domination in the name of God would again be front and center on the pages of history.

Today, traditional American Christians are finding the notion of living an "upright and holy life before God" even more difficult, as the culture wars and the returning surge of secularism[14] continues to change the core values of a new generation.

Prayer in schools—even the Pledge of Allegiance—are all but forgotten traits of a former generation. Political pundits on both sides of the argument now find themselves in a struggle for the sake of determining, not whether a nation believes "In God We Trust," but whether there is any reason to trust anyone at all.

---

14. http://time.com/4385755/faith-in-america/

PART FOUR
IT WILL BE FAIR WEATHER

"When it is evening, ye say, It will be fair weather: for the sky is red. And in the morning, It will be foul weather to day: for the sky is red and lowering. O ye hypocrites, ye can discern the face of the sky; but can ye not discern the signs of the times? A wicked and adulterous generation seeketh after a sign; and there shall no sign be given unto it."

—Matthew 16

Prosperity, popularity, and poverty make strange bedfellows. But in any society, all three are ever-present and often become key influences in the long-term survival of a people.

The pages of the Old and New Testaments suggest that the intersection between God's favoring the Jews and His turning to the Gentile nations for their redemption set in motion a series of global evolutionary events that have continued to serve as both unifier as well as disrupter for cultures and faiths all around the world for 2,000 years. Signs of the times, as it were, have been all around us.[1]

1. https://www.christianstudylibrary.org/article/signs-times-1

History has shown that wealth and affluence breed greater levels of pride and fuels the pride cycle even more. While wickedness and carnal chaos are often balanced in religious discourse with overcoming economic struggle and persecution, one surefire indication of this being the last dispensation is to check those ancient signs against the moral condition of the civilizations of today's world.

Mankind has progressed through deep tracts of pestilence, anguish, and struggle. As a world economy, and perhaps with more favorable circumstances for some nations over others, human society has experienced a level of prosperity, opportunity, and success in advances in science, technology, and medicine—all posing a challenge of one form or another on the conflict between the spiritual welfare and social evolution of mankind. Although no real indicator of success, the prosperity of the human race is at an all-time high, including nearly 6,000 individuals with more than $1 billion in wealth and nearly 60 million individuals classified as "millionaires."[2] Paul hinted that things might go well, if we but follow the words of Christ:

> And this same God who takes care of me will supply all your needs from his glorious riches, which have been given to us in Christ Jesus. (Philippians 4)

During His mortal ministry, Jesus warned His disciples to be cautious of those who would try to sway them into thinking they were directed by Him and that an elevated status in life would influence the gullible among the flock. In Matthew, the writer records Jesus as saying many will come to deceive and that being rich doesn't guarantee passage into God's presence:

> If thou wilt be perfect, go and sell that thou hast, and give to the poor, and thou shalt have treasure in heaven: and come and follow me. . . . Verily I say unto you, That a rich man shall hardly enter into the kingdom of heaven. . . . It is easier for a camel to go through

---

2. https://www.forbes.com/billionaires/

> the eye of a needle, than for a rich man to enter into the kingdom of God. (Matthew 19)

By the middle of the fourteenth century, as the Dark Ages reached their dimmest period, the world was losing between one-third and one-half of the entire human race to the "black death." This was the second pandemic that impacted Europe, with the great plague of 541—often referred to as the Plague of Justinian[3]—which claimed 45 percent of the entire Roman Empire, from Egypt to Constantinople. No amount of wealth or power could stop the world from suffering.

If the reassurance of a world devastated, overcome by fire and damnation, doesn't pose enough incentive for the human race to call itself to some higher form of spiritual order, the writer of Ecclesiastes also reminds us that there are no second chances, and we don't get to take anything with us:

> If thou seest the oppression of the poor, and violent perverting of judgment and justice in a province, marvel not at the matter: for he that is higher than the highest regardeth; and there be higher than they. . . . He that loveth silver shall not be satisfied with silver; nor he that loveth abundance with increase: this is also vanity. . . . As he came forth of his mother's womb, naked shall he return to go as he came, and shall take nothing of his labour, which he may carry away in his hand. (Ecclesiastes 5)

In his many letters to the young Church of Christ, Paul reminded those from a myriad of backgrounds, economic stations, and scores of tongues and traditions that just as Jesus lived one life to atone for the human race, so shall all of us only get one chance at mortality:

> But now once in the end of the world hath he appeared to put away sin by the sacrifice of himself. And as it is appointed unto men once to die, but after this the judgment: So Christ was once offered to bear the sins of many; and unto them that look for him shall he appear the second time without sin unto salvation. (Hebrews 9)

---

3. Understanding the Plague of Justinian

Just as there will be readers of this work who will speculate, conjecture, and criticize what has been offered as merely one writer's perspectives on the threads of eschatology, so too have there always been cynics who have chosen to deny the signs of the times. In the time of ancient Israel, even in the presence of great miracles and the appearances of angels, God's children often doubted the signs of the times:

> Therefore, the people came to Moses, and said, We have sinned, for we have spoken against the Lord, and against thee; pray unto the Lord, that he take away the serpents from us. . . . And Moses made a serpent of brass, and put it upon a pole, and it came to pass, that if a serpent had bitten any man, when he beheld the serpent of brass, he lived. (Numbers 21)

Time and again, despite the examples and warnings, mankind has had a problem believing what we read, hear about, and even see. In the case of the so-called "brazen serpent" on top of the staff of Moses, it, rather than the faith it represented, became an object of worship to which even Judah's king, Hezekiah, had destroyed 500 years later:

> Hezekiah the son of Ahaz king of Judah began to reign. . . . And he did that which was right in the sight of the Lord, according to all that David his father did. He removed the high places, and brake the images, and cut down the groves, and brake in pieces the brasen serpent that Moses had made: for unto those days the children of Israel did burn incense to it: and he called it Nehushtan. (2 Kings 18)

The Bible offers many examples of ancient times in which those chosen to do God's work were abandoned, abused, persecuted, and put to death, despite the signs. Isaiah, one of the most outspoken prophets of his time, foretold of a coming Redeemer who would save the world from itself:

- Heaven will give the sign of a babe being born to a virgin (Isaiah 7:14)
- His heritage will come through the house of David (Isaiah 9:7).

- His way will be prepared before him by John the Baptist, His cousin (Isaiah 40:3).
- He will make a blood atonement (Isaiah 53:5).
- He will bear the sins and sorrows of all of us (Isaiah 53:4).
- He will be buried in the tomb of a wealthy man (Isaiah 53:9).
- He will judge the world in righteousness (Isaiah 11:4).

Despite the promptings of a great prophet, as well as the forewarnings of those who followed Isaiah, the children of Israel continued to ignore the signs given them.

In His time with the Pharisees, Jesus reproached them for not identifying the biblical signs that had foreshadowed the times they were living in:

> He answered and said unto them, When it is evening, ye say, It will be fair weather: for the sky is red. And in the morning, It will be foul weather today: for the sky is red and lowering. O ye hypocrites, ye can discern the face of the sky; but can ye not discern the signs of the times? (Matthew 16)

While the Pharisees and Sadducees were attempting to trap Jesus in a sort of double-jeopardy compromise, like generations before in Noah's time, Jesus used the analogy of the weather to predict the coming of difficult times. As in the time of Noah, although from God's point of view, and a few of his faithful followers, the impending storm clouds heralded the coming rains that consumed just about everyone—all the while, the people, like the Pharisees and Sadducees, ignored the warnings:

> For as in the days that were before the flood they were eating and drinking, marrying and giving in marriage, until the day that Noe entered into the ark, And knew not until the flood came, and took them all away; so shall also the coming of the Son of man be. (Matthew 24)

Another of His poignant prophecies was that His gospel would be preached throughout the world before he would return:

> And this gospel of the kingdom shall be preached in all the world for a witness unto all nations; and then shall the end come. (Matthew 24)

Among the 195 countries of the world,[4] and the seven billion people who live here, the Christian population has quadrupled[5] over the past century alone. More than two billion people claim some form of Christian principle as a core tenet of their religion. While the entire Western Hemisphere is predominantly Christian,[6] the spread of the word of Christ throughout Southern and Central Africa, Eastern

---

4. https://www.worldometers.info/geography/how-many-countries-are-there-in-the-world/#:~:text=Countries%20in%twentiethe%20World%3A&text=There%20are%20195%20countries%20in,and%twentiethe%20State%20of%20Palestine.
5. http://www.pewforum.org/2011/12/19/global-christianity-exec/
6. https://www.washingtonpost.com/news/worldviews/wp/2012/12/18/our-christian-earth-the-astounding-reach-of-the-worlds-largest-religion-in-charts-and-maps/?noredirect=on&utm_term=.3aa5b1cad1da
   https://billygraham.org/answer/why-are-people-losing-faith-in-god/
   https://www.gotquestions.org/great-apostasy.html
   https://www.theatlantic.com/magazine/archive/1919/07/a-jewish-palestine/303393/
   https://www.thegospelcoalition.org/article/9-things-you-should-know-about-rabbinic-judaism/
   http://www.jewishencyclopedia.com/articles/7535-hellenism
   http://www.mcgill.ca/classics/files/classics/2006-7-07.pdf
   http://www.bible.ca/archeology/bible-archeology-samaritans.htm
   https://www.britannica.com/place/Caesarea
   https://www.ligonier.org/learn/devotionals/the-church-in-antioch/
   http://ringofchrist.com/early-christian-history/
   http://www.biblestudy.org/apostlepaul/life-epistles-of-apostle-paul/iconium-lystra-derbe.html
   https://www.biblicalarchaeology.org/daily/biblical-sites-places/biblical-archaeology-sites/church-of-laodicea-in-the-bible-and-archaeology/
   https://www.thoughtco.com/miletus-greek-history-119714
   https://www.ancient.eu/ephesos/
   http://bibleatlas.org/assos.htm
   https://www.ancient.eu/Philippi/
   https://www.ancient.eu/Greek_Religion/
   http://bibleatlas.org/corinth.htm
   https://bbhchurchconnection.wordpress.com/2015/01/09/how-immoral-was-corinth-really/
   https://www.biblestudytools.com/history/joseph-barber-lightfoot-biblical-essays/the-church-of-thessalonica.html

Europe, and Northern Asia are seeing steady increases in those who believe in the story of Jesus and His ministry.

The long, dark journey of Christianity from the time of Peter, James, John, Paul, and Jesus up to today has seen anything but "fair weather," as tribulation, adversity, nobility, and triumph have continued to refine the faithful and confound the skeptical.

---

https://www.encyclopedia.com/philosophy-and-religion/ancient-religions/ancient-religion/cabiri

https://www.ancient.eu/Roman_Religion/

https://courses.lumenlearning.com/suny-hccc-worldhistory/chapter/diocletian-and-the-tetrarchy/

https://www.theregister.co.uk/2006/10/06/the_odd_body_religion/

http://www.pewforum.org/2011/12/19/global-christianity-exec/

https://www.washingtonpost.com/news/worldviews/wp/2012/12/18/our-christian-earth-the-astounding-reach-of-the-worlds-largest-religion-in-charts-and-maps/?noredirect=on&utm_term=.3aa5b1cad1da

CHAPTER NINE
DISTRESS IN THE LAND

> *"For there shall be great distress in the land, and wrath upon this people. And they shall fall by the edge of the sword, and shall be led away captive into all nations: . . . And there shall be signs in the sun, and in the moon, and in the stars; and upon the earth distress of nations, with perplexity; the sea and the waves roaring; Men's hearts failing them for fear, and for looking after those things which are coming on the earth: for the powers of heaven shall be shaken."*
>
> —Luke 21

Pandemonium is a scary word. When English writer John Milton wrote his magnum opus, *Paradise Lost*, in 1667, he invented a word that combined the Greek word for "all" (*pan*) and the Latin reference to an evil deity (*daemonium*),[1] to describe the devil's dwelling place.[2]

Today, a similar term—*pandemic*—is used to describe a massive outbreak of disease that spreads rampantly throughout the human

1. https://worldofdictionary.com/dict/latin-english/meaning/daemonium
2. http://www.wordorigins.org/index.php/site/pandemonium/

race, like the one gripping the world right now.[3] By consequence, whenever such a pandemic, such as this one or the Spanish flu in 1917, regardless of time, place, or economic circumstances, pandemonium usually follows.[4]

While speaking from the Mount of Olives, Jesus pointed to a time in which the pandemic of illnesses would burden the people of the earth, as a sign of the end of times, and prior to His return:

> And ye shall hear of wars and rumours of wars: see that ye be not troubled: for all these things must come to pass, but the end is not yet . . . and there shall be famines, and pestilences, and earthquakes, in divers places. All these are the beginning of sorrows. (Matthew 24)

Welcome to now!

In the last days prior to His return, and in spite of medical developments, the Lord foretells of a time in which mankind will suffer from diseases and pestilences of unimaginable scope and magnitude:

> Great earthquakes shall be in divers places, and famines, and pestilences; and fearful sights and great signs shall there be from heaven. . . . Men's hearts failing them for fear, and for looking after those things which are coming on the earth. . . . And then shall they see the Son of man coming in a cloud with power and great glory. (Luke 21)

In the Apostle John's vision of God's kingdom, as accounted in Revelation, John saw four beasts that would be assigned to oversee the woes of mankind. Christian legend holds that these four creatures described in John's vision held the seals of famine, war, pestilence, and death.[5]

---

3. https://academic.oup.com/jid/article/200/7/1018/903237
4. https://www.nejm.org/doi/full/10.1056/NEJM198303173081105
5. https://www.britannica.com/topic/four-horsemen-of-the-Apocalypse

A common visual depiction of one of John's prophecies in Revelation refers to his vision of the four seals of the feared "Horsemen of the Apocalypse":[6]

> When the Lamb opened one of the seals, and I heard, as it were the noise of thunder, one of the four beasts saying, Come and see. And I saw, and behold a white horse: and he that sat on him had a bow; and a crown was given unto him: and he went forth conquering, and to conquer. . . . And there went out another horse that was red: and power was given to him that sat thereon to take peace from the earth . . . heard the third beast say, Come and see. And I beheld, and lo a black horse; and he that sat on him had a pair of balances in his hand. . . . And when he had opened the fourth seal, I heard the voice of the fourth beast. . . . And I looked and behold a pale horse: and his name that sat on him was Death, and Hell followed with him. (Revelation 6)

Perhaps one of the more telling signs of the times is the rise of what were once thought to be abolished illnesses,[7] including the plague, measles, and rubella, not to mention the growing medical concerns surrounding AIDS, opioid abuse, and a variety of exotic illnesses with limited or no apparent countermeasures.

According to medical studies, physicians now advise the public on a regular basis of the resurgence of disease that is evolving into drug-resistant strains,[8] including tuberculosis and polio, which were once thought eradicated from society. With the easy access to antibiotics and strong over-the-counter remedies, combined with the driving revenues being exploited by large medical providers, critics suggest that the world is becoming a potential petri dish for powerful new strains of illnesses with the potential of wiping out most of us.

This new pandemic, COVID-19, for example, has evolved despite medical attention to evade the human immune system, further

---

6. http://www.newworldencyclopedia.org/entry/Four_Horsemen_of_the_Apocalypse
7. http://www.health.com/childhood-vaccines/5-old-diseases-that-are-making-a-comeback
8. http://time.com/27308/4-diseases-making-a-comeback-thanks-to-anti-vaxxers/

establishing the potential for another global pandemic similar to those from recent history, in which the power of science continues to battle the forces of nature.

Only a century ago, between 20 and 50 million people succumbed to the Spanish flu,[9] which had a fatality rate of between 15 and 20 percent. Compared with the Spanish flu of 1918,[10] the current strain of H7N9 avian virus, which has been known to spark into epidemic potential more frequently than has been expected by medical researchers, has a fatality rate of almost 30 percent. Such a pandemic—some analysts suggest—is more of a matter of "when" rather than "if," which might suggest the current situation with COVID-19 being far milder in comparison to what is foretold.

Scientists call attention to the fact that we live in the Information Age,[11] and the potential impetus for the increase in the risk of a pandemic is due to our trade, travel, and connectivity.[12] The increased risk of a pandemic of "extinction" is looming in the shadows of medical research, some researchers suggest, despite our efforts to improve on preventive medicine.

In any given year, various forms of diseases (called "aoontes") are transferred between animals and humans, according to the Center for Disease Control.[13] Two factors come into play, based on medical studies, including the level of exposure we have to animals in general and the density of our populations. Other factors, including medical issues (receptor compatibility, mutations and survivability, and so on), are considered when determining the potential spread of a disease. Moreover, each year, more than 200 strains of cancer,[14] from a combination of factors including heavy elements in our air and from

9. https://www.history.com/topics/1918-flu-pandemic
10. https://virus.stanford.edu/uda/
11. https://expectexceptional.economist.com/managing-pandemics-with-data.html
12. https://www.vox.com/2016/5/31/11638796/why-there-are-more-infectious-disease-outbreaks
13. https://www.cdc.gov/onehealth/basics/zoonotic-diseases.html
14. http://www.cancerresearchuk.org/about-cancer/coping/physically/how-can-cancer-kill-you

exhaust fumes, tobacco, as well as toxic chemicals in food and water, and exposure to the sun, take the lives of more than 7 million people.[15]

COVID-19, which came to existence in a short period of time, has changed the landscape of the world on so many levels: how we communicate, where we travel, what we wear. Even political lines have been drawn regarding the disease, its impact, and the corresponding efficacy of treating it with mandatory medical support. And it continues to be a prolific problem for many nations and in the case of some types of people (including the elderly and the sick):

> And power was given unto them over the fourth part of the earth, to kill with sword, and with hunger, and with death, and with the beasts of the earth. . . . Then I heard a loud voice from the temple, saying to the seven angels, "Go and pour out on the earth the seven bowls of the wrath of God." So, the first angel went and poured out his bowl on the earth; and it became a loathsome and malignant sore on the people who had the mark of the beast and who worshiped his image. The second angel poured out his bowl into the sea, and it became blood like that of a dead man; and every living thing in the sea died. (Revelation 6, 16)

What, then, if anything, should the human race do to prepare as such dire times may be upon us? Christian leaders, religious scholars,[16] and eschatologists might agree that the countermeasures for surviving such a terrible and inevitable blight on mankind is also outlined among more than forty separate warnings and prophecies throughout the Old and New Testaments: [17]

> Because thou hast made the Lord, which is my refuge, even the most high, thy habitation; There shall no evil befall thee, neither shall any plague come nigh thy dwelling. . . . But unto you that fear my name shall the Sun of righteousness arise with healing in

15. http://www.worldcancerday.org/world-cancer-day-2013-global-press-release
16. http://www.biblelineministries.org/articles/basearch.php?action=full&mainkey=PESTILENCES+-+A+SIGN
17. https://bible.knowing-jesus.com/topics/Plagues

> his wings; and ye shall go forth and grow up as calves of the stall. (Psalm 91; Malachi 4)

In 2004, a survey was conducted in which 1,100 physicians were interviewed by the Jewish Theological Seminary in New York. More than 70 percent of those physicians believe miracles occur beyond their respective prognosis, and more than half of the physicians considered that medical practice should be directed by religious conviction (either patient or doctor).[18]

Based on what John sees for the future of the human race, and what the world is experiencing right now, that sounds like good medicine!

---

18. https://journalofethics.ama-assn.org/article/lord-i-need-healing-uneasy-relationship-between-faith-and-medicine/2005-05

Chapter Ten
Run to and fro

"And they that be wise shall shine as the brightness of the firmament; and they that turn many to righteousness as the stars for ever and ever. But thou, O Daniel, shut up the words, and seal the book, even to the time of the end: many shall run to and fro, and knowledge shall be increased."

—Daniel 12

Few things illustrate mortality better than jumping off a cliff without a parachute or trying to walk on water (like someone else we know!). But there's more to the scientific laws surrounding gravity than what Isaac Newton postulated in the seventeenth century.

Discoveries expanding how we see the laws of gravity and other physical properties in science required time and the evolution of scientific thought, as well as the advancement of technology and how to apply it to the laws of physics.

When the English scientist Sir Isaac Newton discovered the relationship between the moon's movement being tied to the movement of an object falling to Earth without constraint, Newton's research and applied theories in physics established the precedent for how we look (literally!) at the weight of the world.[1] Technology and the progression of scientific reasoning in our time have grown exponentially almost since the beginning of the twentieth century.

One of the significant signs of man heading toward terminal velocity on our path through mortality, eschatologists say, is the advancement of technology and science that will outpace human development itself. For many Christian scholars, that time Daniel pointed to as the time in which "many shall run to and fro, and knowledge shall increase,"[2] is now coming to pass.

Often referred to as the Father of Experimental Philosophy, Sir Francis Bacon, along with Newton, became instrumental in establishing scientific inductive reasoning[3] as part of the fabric of modern thinking in the seventeenth century. In his epic *Novum Organum*,[4] or *New Instrumentation*,[5] Bacon suggested ideas of how human knowledge and scientific thought regarding natural and unexplainable phenomena should be classified into empirical groupings based on facts, hypotheses, or an absence of logic:

> It is idle to expect any great advancement in science from the superinducing and engrafting of new things upon old. We must begin anew from the very foundations, unless we would revolve forever in a circle with mean and contemptible progress. (Sir Francis Bacon [1620])

Bacon's introduction of the scientific method began a 300-year revolution in transforming modern society from a traditionally religious-centered culture to one based on science and logical reasoning for the unexplained. This Age of Enlightenment[6] produced volumes of writings, new forms of music, refined scientific instrumentation,

---

1. https://answersingenesis.org/creation-scientists/misplaced-faith-isaac-newton/
2. https://www.kingjamesbibleonline.org/1611_Daniel-Chapter-12/
3. https://www.livescience.com/21569-deduction-vs-induction.html
4. https://study.com/academy/lesson/novum-organum-by-sir-francis-bacon-summary-analysis.html
5. https://www.britannica.com/science/Baconian-method#ref127745
6. https://www.history.com/topics/enlightenment

inventions, and advancements in military science that ultimately led to the nuclear age.

French writer/philosopher Voltaire[7] supposed that the equality of humanity was based exclusively on empirical reasoning, as he implied in his satirical perspective on religious philosophies and excessive living by faith and idealism, Candide.[8] A contemporary of Newton, Voltaire believed that it wasn't fate or faith that determined the outcomes of society but the will and reasoning of an inventive mind and looking after one's own domestic follies:

> It is demonstrable . . . that things cannot be otherwise than as they are; for all being created for an end, all is necessarily for the best end. Observe, that the nose has been formed to bear spectacles—thus we have spectacles. Legs are visibly designed for stockings—and we have stockings. Stones were made to be hewn, and to construct castles—therefore my lord has a magnificent castle; for the greatest baron in the province ought to be the best lodged. Pigs were made to be eaten—therefore we eat pork all the year round. Consequently, they who assert that all is well have said a foolish thing, they should have said all is for the best. (Voltaire [Candide])

With traditional belief systems beginning to change as the Protestant Reformation was settling into the status quo, new perspectives on the nature of God and His relationship with mankind began to emerge. Many prominent minds of the Enlightenment period would even start to question the need to believe in a higher deity. Christians suggest this too was foreseen by the prophets of old, including Paul's admonition to one of his principal his pupils:

> O Timothy, keep that which is committed to thy trust, avoiding profane and vain babblings, and oppositions of science falsely so called: Which some professing have erred concerning the faith. (1 Timothy 6)

---

7. https://plato.stanford.edu/entries/voltaire/
8. https://www.britannica.com/topic/Candide-by-Voltaire

Through the Age of Enlightenment, Christians have seen a sort of ironic twist that in the Age of Reason, matters concerning prayer, divine revelation, and the very life and biblical account surrounding Jesus Christ border on the ridiculous. The laws of man, scientists reasoned, should be governed not by an invisible God but rather through the laws of science.

Today, in a more secularized society than in the past, the notion of science and technology being used to explain away faith appears in almost every aspect of modern life, and—some scholars speculate—further make the case of the Psalmists, Isaiah, Paul and others:

> The heavens declare the glory of God; and the firmament sheweth his handywork. Day unto day uttereth speech, and night unto night sheweth knowledge . . . when they knew God, they glorified him not as God, neither were thankful; but became vain in their imaginations, and their foolish heart was darkened. Professing themselves to be wise, they became fools, and changed the glory of the uncorruptible God into an image made like to corruptible man. (Psalm 19; Romans 1)

With the mapping of the human genome, chemically developed test tube babies, cloning, advanced DNA sequencing, and the blending of science and human development, scientific advancement has done much to extend the perception that the laws of nature are the only ones that should warrant thoughtful consideration. Although the scientific advancements throughout the past 350 years have seen the juxtaposition between human extinction by natural causes and man-made catastrophe, millions of souls whose faith is not founded in exposure to spiritual experiences are now more inclined to be dismissive of anything relating to God and the mystique that follows the principals of faith and the belief in miracles:

> For the invisible things of him from the creation of the world are clearly seen, being understood by the things that are made, even his eternal power and Godhead; so that they are without excuse. (Romans 1)

Perhaps one final telling sign of the times that further points to a confluence between technology and prophecy lies with the insight John shared in Revelation, in which he foresees a period of tribulation that will blur the lines between morality and technology—a time in which machines described as "locusts" and "scorpions" would be brought into battle:

> And the shapes of the locusts were like unto horses prepared unto battle; and on their heads were as it were crowns like gold, and their faces were as the faces of men. And they had hair as the hair of women, and their teeth were as the teeth of lions. And they had breastplates, as it were breastplates of iron; and the sound of their wings was as the sound of chariots of many horses running to battle. And they had tails like unto scorpions, and there were stings in their tails: and their power was to hurt men. (Revelation 9)

Without argument, the study of and advancement of science and technology have brought further knowledge, understanding, and inspiration about the human condition and how to improve life as we know it. From such influences as Copernicus, Galileo (who challenged the traditional status quo on the nature of the earth and the sun and their respective relationship to one another), to Charles Darwin and his *Origin of Species*, biology, physics, math, and engineering all point to knowledge being something that evolves the way in which the human race looks at its existence, well beyond the "Big Bang" that occurred, according to scientists, 14 billion years ago:

> A knowledge of the existence of something we cannot penetrate, of the manifestations of the profoundest reason and the most radiant beauty—it is this knowledge and this emotion that constitute the truly religious attitude. (Albert Einstein)

At the conclusion of His counsel to His apostles from the Mount of Olives, and shortly before He retreated to a nearby garden to atone for the sins of the human race, Jesus offered a warning and a loving bit of advice for those who would believe on His purpose. It is in His words that there may be no better way to conclude this section:

Heaven and earth shall pass away: but my words shall not pass away. And take heed to yourselves, lest at any time your hearts be overcharged with surfeiting, and drunkenness, and cares of this life, and so that day come upon you unawares. For as a snare shall it come on all them that dwell on the face of the whole earth.

Watch ye therefore, and pray always, that ye may be accounted worthy to escape all these things that shall come to pass, and to stand before the Son of man. (Matthew 24)

Part Five
Seek and Find Me

"Thus saith the Lord of hosts, the God of Israel, unto all that are carried away captives, whom I have caused to be carried away from Jerusalem unto Babylon; Build ye houses, and dwell in them; and plant gardens, and eat the fruit of them; And seek the peace of the city whither I have caused you to be carried away captives, and pray unto the Lord for it: for in the peace thereof shall ye have peace . . . and ye shall seek me, and find me, when ye shall search for me with all your heart."

—Jeremiah 29

When was the first time you read a good book? Many people might think that books were first printed and distributed by Johannes Gutenberg, because of his advancements surrounding the printing press in the mid-1400s in Germany.

While it must be acknowledged that Johannes Gutenberg's new technology helped introduce the word of God (as well as everything else that was printed at the time) to the West, the process of moveable type had been long established throughout Asia. In China, by the second century, craftsmen were imbedding ink onto paper using blocks, and by the mid-800s, their technology was advanced enough to produce complete publications.

While historians and scholars continue to debate the intent, origins, and motives behind Gutenberg's work (he was never paid for the 180 copies of his Bible), most agree that the work surrounding what is now one of the most valuable and rare historical documents in the world[1] laid the groundwork for what would become the Age of Enlightenment.[2]

By the end of the Middle Ages, which is usually marked by the fall of Constantinople in 1453, Christianity was so much the part of the fabric of Western culture that there was little distinction between "community" and "religion." Everything was influenced and aligned with the Church—whether music, or art—even science.

But it was literature and the distribution of the written word that scholars suggest had the fastest influence on advancing Western thought following the Dark Ages. The leading publication, of course, was that of the Bible. Monks were producing illuminated copies of various passages throughout the fourteenth and fifteenth centuries to help spread the word of God to places where it had not yet been introduced.

Gutenberg's work with moveable type led to the new concept of mass communication, a concept that forever altered the way in which societies and civilizations would develop, and how people learned, discussed, and believed:

> It is a press, certainly, but a press from which shall flow in inexhaustible streams, the most abundant and most marvelous liquor that has ever flowed to relieve the thirst of men! Through it, God will spread His Word. A spring of truth shall flow from it: like a new star it shall scatter the darkness of ignorance, and

1. Currently there are only 21 complete copies of the Gutenberg Bible in existence, with an estimated value north of $30 million. Individual pages of the 75-pound book currently fetch between $50,000 and $150,000, depending on which page and its quality.
2. https://www.history.com/topics/british-history/enlightenment

cause a light heretofore unknown to shine amongst men. (Johannes Gutenberg)[3]

The written word reorganizes insights about how concepts regarding life, liberty, property—even God—are perceived, believed, and acted upon. As new concepts in how things are perceived were distributed, those "in-the-know" begin to expand, and where only wealthy religious leaders and royal families had been in control of ideas, a sense of reformation began to take hold of central Europe, largely in part because of mass communication. Throughout the fifteenth and sixteenth centuries, as self-awareness began to reshape the way people looked at their respective leaders both in the church and in their local governments, a sense of nationalism began to grow, as the elitists who had been in control were now on even plains of understanding with commoners.

In a way, one might say that the world had an "epiphany" and was inspired by the likes of a new means of communicating. For early Christians, the "epiphany," or epiphanaeia,[4] represented not only the birth of Christ but also His return in glory. Conversely, Judaism contends that the whole idea of a "Second Coming" is little more than a ruse contrived by dissatisfied Christians (and displaced Jews).[5] Why couldn't Jesus, they argue, get what He needed done during His mortal ministry (including saving them from the Romans)?

Like those many prophets who were sent by His Father before Him, Jesus made extra effort to warn even His enemies of the impending time of their demise. In what has become known throughout the Christian world as the Olivet Discourse,[6] Jesus foretold of a time that the temple would be destroyed, His followers persecuted for His name's sake, and that—like the surety of the temple being rebuilt

3. https://www.britannica.com/topic/Academic-American-Encyclopedia; accessed Oct. 2014.
4. http://www.plainerwords.com/artman2/publish/2007/Epiphaneia.shtml
5. https://www.jpost.com/blogs/the-jewish-problem---from-anti-judaism-to-anti-semitism/christian-insecurity-the-problem-of-the-second-coming-381034
6. https://ca.thegospelcoalition.org/columns/ad-fontes/making-sense-olivet-discourse/

in the last days—He too would be resurrected and would eventually return in glory:

> And Jesus answering said unto him, Seest thou these great buildings? there shall not be left one stone upon another, that shall not be thrown down. . . . And the gospel must first be published among all nations. . . . For false Christs and false prophets shall rise, and shall shew signs and wonders, to seduce, if it were possible, even the elect. Take heed that no man deceive you. For many shall come in my name, saying, I am Christ; and shall deceive many. . . . And many false prophets shall rise and shall deceive many. And because iniquity shall abound, the love of many shall wax cold. . . . Settle it therefore in your hearts, not to meditate before what ye shall answer: For I will give you a mouth and wisdom, which all your adversaries shall not be able to gainsay nor resist. And ye shall be hated of all men for my name's sake... But in those days, after that tribulation, the sun shall be darkened, and the moon shall not give her light, and the stars of heaven shall fall, and the powers that are in heaven shall be shaken. And then shall they see the Son of man coming in the clouds with great power and glory. (Mark 13; Matthew 24; Luke 21)

Continuing with our "pride cycle," we find ourselves in the phase in which the pangs of humility become a dominant force in humanity's desire to improve the odds of not becoming self-consuming through hubris and self-interest.

If the reassurance of a devastated world succumbed by raining fire and damnation doesn't pose enough incentive for mortal man to get his spiritual self in order, modern doctrine as taught by some Christian faiths also teaches that there will be no second chances. If people don't prepare to meet God in this life, it will be too late in the next life:[7]

> And as it is appointed unto men once to die, but after this the judgment: . . . Whereas ye know not what shall be on the morrow.

7. https://anothercity.org/is-there-no-repentance-after-death-2/

> For what is your life? It is even a vapour, that appeareth for a little time, and then vanisheth away. (Hebrews 9; James 4)

The post-medieval Roman Catholic Church in the sixteenth century was rife with controversy—thanks in part to the ability of commoners learning to read and who no longer chose to follow one singular (and often mandated) frame of thought about how things should run in life, in the fields, and in church. The notion of "western capitalism" began to take root in Europe in the early 1500s, which gave new light to how people saw their lives meaning something more than fodder for the fiefdoms.[8]

Throughout sixteenth-century Europe, the spread of doubt over the teachings of the church began to take hold among the religious scholars and influencers. Some religious historians suggest the impetus behind the rise in controversy is tied to translations of the original texts—specifically those by fourth-century Christian philosopher Augustine—as well as others from the early church.

Throughout the prior 1500 years, the church—especially with respect to the Pope, his cardinals, and their respective lieutenants—had swayed the government landscape throughout Europe. The subsequent conspiracies and partisan influences, combined with the dramatic rise in power, wealth, and control by Rome, ultimately led to the church's authority being compromised, which resulted in its loss of control over the spiritual component of life for many disaffected parishioners.

A rise in financial abuse because of the pedaling of spiritual liberties and absolutions called "indulgences" led to mass corruption as well, further expanding the schism between the faithful and the leadership.

The Protestant Reformation had taken hold of central Europe by 1521 and spread from the Baltic to the Atlantic, with the newfound Lutheranism becoming the state religion of Germany in 1524, as well as throughout the Scandinavian states.

8. https://www.britannica.com/topic/history-of-Europe/The-emergence-of-modern-Europe-1500-1648

With the rapid spread of the Reformation throughout Europe during the mid-sixteenth century, Lutheranism spawned other protestant factions, including Anabaptists, who condemned the practice of infant baptism, Calvinists, who believed in the philosophy of predestination, and Socinians,[9] who protested the original doctrine on the Holy Trinity. Despite the growing range in controversy surrounding the church, which ranged from ambivalence to outright rebellion, and the rise in support for the shift in religious thought led by the likes of Calvin and Luther notwithstanding, the Catholic Church did (and still does) remain a bulwark for spiritual strength for millions of followers.

By the mid-1500s, while the Greek Orthodox faction of Catholicism controlled much of Greece and Eastern Europe, the religious influence over intellectual, religious, and political thought by Rome throughout central and western Europe was weakening as other issues emerged as more impactful on society. European nobility and gentry amassed large tracts of land, replete with serfs that were dedicated to serving the land, more so than a non-corporeal deity.[10] Pondering on human mortality was something taken for granted, given the constant fear of the plague, inter-kingdom rivalries, and other life-shortening situations that were ever-present.

But for the righteous faithful—many who followed God's law (as they would discover it)—the afterlife won't all be about diseases and strife, any more than it will be about sitting on clouds, playing with our harps and halos. There will be much work to do for those who were obedient, we just have to find our way back.

9. https://www.newadvent.org/cathen/14113a.htm
10. https://www.britannica.com/topic/history-of-Europe/The-economic-background

Chapter Eleven
Neither Will I Hide My Face

"And it shall come to pass afterward, that I will pour out my spirit upon all flesh; and your sons and your daughters shall prophesy, your old men shall dream dreams, your young men shall see visions. . . . Neither will I hide my face any more from them: for I have poured out my spirit upon the house of Israel, saith the Lord God."

—Joel 2; Ezekiel 39

Our world finds itself in the early half of the twenty-first century, with the news of the day revealing, more often than not, new scientific and technological advances that have been otherwise only thought of as science fiction—in medicine, communications, nuclear science, and conflict. But in the adolescence of the "2000s," amidst torrential destruction, firestorms, and an abundance of "rumors of war," the wisest among us have always turned to signs in history to foresee the signs of the times. Cars race to beyond 200 miles per hour, aircraft fly beyond five times the speed of sound, and man has reached other planets and has learned to harness the power of a single atom.

Our ability to progress to greater levels of knowledge and understanding is enhanced by our willingness to accept the possibility that we don't know everything and that the will of the Lord, while offered only in glimpses, needed to be removed and restored to the earth, as was prophesied by the likes of Isaiah, Amos, Matthew, and Jesus Himself:

> Watch and pray, lest you enter into temptation. The spirit indeed is willing, but the flesh is weak. . . . Take heed that no man deceive you. For many shall come in my name, saying, I am Christ; and shall deceive many. . . . For nation shall rise against nation, and kingdom against kingdom: and there shall be famines, and pestilences, and earthquakes, in divers places. . . . And many false prophets shall rise and shall deceive many. (Matthew 24)

Now, in a time of "increased knowledge" when nations continue to rise against nations, continuing to find and follow the word of God while subsequently trying (in vain) to forecast the great and dreadful day of the Lord has become something of a punch line for an increasingly secular society.

But rewind a couple of millennia and we discover that the companionship of the written word, which was preserved only for the prominent figures of the religious community, was a far simpler tome.

Well into establishing the Roman empire, the known population of "God's children" held to the first five books of the Old Testament as the single volume of divine revelation, and that body of work would be the core tenet on which Judaism would hang its perspective and doctrine of the relationship between God and man. But then Jesus showed up in Jerusalem, and the whole God-fearing world was turned upside down. With the onset of Jesus's ministry and the subsequent witnesses and admonitions by His Apostles, the children of God found new words of inspiration, even a new set of commandments:

> It is not for you to know the times or the seasons, which the Father hath put in his own power. But ye shall receive power, after that the Holy Ghost is come upon you: and ye shall be witnesses unto me both in Jerusalem, and in all Judaea, and in Samaria, and unto the uttermost part of the earth. . . . And while they looked steadfastly toward heaven as he went up, behold, two men stood by them in white apparel; Which also said, Ye men of Galilee, why stand ye gazing up into heaven? this same Jesus, which is taken up from you

> into heaven, shall so come in like manner as ye have seen him go into heaven. (Acts 1)

Such words, which Jesus left behind upon His ascension into heaven, were always revealed under the direction of one of the Lord's authorized witnesses and inspired by the Holy Ghost.

The Holy Bible provides an early record of not only the "children of God" but also foreshadows and testifies of the life and times of Jesus Christ. The Bible has influenced the Christian world for hundreds of generations. Its many historical accounts span from the beginning of man, through the life of Christ, and into our future. Buried in the many biblical iterations and interpretations are found important aspects that serve as spiritual pointers to what some Christian sects believe to be indications of a spiritual drought caused by the absence of God's kingdom on earth but with the promise of its restoration.

The Old Testament includes the body of religious work used by the Jews of ancient times, which was also later accepted by the followers of Christ. Much like the ancient Church, the actual contents of the Bible, however, have varied through the ages,[1] as many interpretations have been made, negotiated, and even fought over. Books contained in the Old Testament were written over centuries of time and assembled from a body of work spanning hundreds of miles, by many authors.

By contrast, the contents of the New Testament came from a few sources and were written during a small period of time, probably within the first 100 years following the life of Jesus, while the ancient Church was still under the direction of his Apostles.

The Old Testament provides the earliest accepted history of God's kingdom on earth. Moses was God's chosen leader around 1500 BC and was the man noted as the principal leader of God's kingdom in the earliest years of His church on the earth. The Old Testament is a collection of books that were written prior to the birth of Jesus, by people who were designated as God's mouthpieces throughout the earliest years of civilized man. These books include testimonials, songs,

1. http://www.greatsite.com/timeline-english-bible-history/

poems, prophecies, and words of instruction. The Old Testament also comprises core doctrine for the original church of God. Modern Christianity consider the Old Testament a critical collection of early views into church government, and prophesy of the coming of the Messiah.

The Old Testament denotes the ancient covenant of Moses, the laws given by God, for the children of Israel. These laws are often considered as the lesser laws[2] because Israel was not spiritually prepared for God's higher laws, which came through His higher "priesthood after the order of Melchizedek," while the New Testament provides an account of the Christian ministries of those who were directly involved in the life and ministry of Jesus, and who were charged to sustain His Church on the earth.

Traditional Christian theology holds that the sacred passages within the Old and New Testaments are literal translations out of the mouth of God Himself. Historical discoveries, hundreds of years of additional manuscripts, research, and further scholarship, however, contend that many of the verses, although inspired and directed by God, in many aspects fall short of being a complete body of divine revelation, as the formal doctrine of Christ was lost in the Great Apostasy at the close of the first century.

Our ability to progress to greater levels of knowledge and understanding is enhanced by our willingness to accept the possibility that we don't know everything and that the will of the Lord, while offered only in glimpses, needed to be removed and restored to the earth, as was prophesied by the likes of Isaiah, Amos, Matthew, and Jesus Himself:

> Watch and pray, lest you enter into temptation. The spirit indeed is willing but the flesh is weak. . . . Take heed that no man deceive you. For many shall come in my name, saying, I am Christ; and shall deceive many. . . . For nation shall rise against nation, and kingdom against kingdom: and there shall be famines, and pestilences, and

2. https://www.lds.org/manual/old-testament-student-manual-genesis-2-samuel/exodus-21-24-31-35-the-mosaic-law-a-preparatory-gospel?lang=eng

> earthquakes, in divers places. . . . And many false prophets shall rise, and shall deceive many. (Matthew 24)

The law of Moses, which preceded the fulfillment of the life of Christ, was to be strictly adhered to as the principal foundation of God's Church on the earth and included the law of "carnal commandments"[3] (worldly commandments that include directions essential to living by the edicts of the day). From a symbolic perspective, these carnal laws could be mapped to the fundamental principles of the gospel of Jesus, which are faith, repentance, baptism by immersion, and receiving the Holy Ghost by one who was authorized to perform this ordinance, holding a specific kind of priesthood:

> For it is evident that our Lord sprang out of Judah; of which tribe Moses spake nothing concerning priesthood. And it is yet far more evident: for that after the similitude of Melchisedec there ariseth another priest, who is made, not after the law of a carnal commandment, but after the power of an endless life. (Hebrews 7)

Moses was tipped off by God that while the two of them were spending quality time in the mountains above Pharaoh's empire, contrary to the order in which they were supposed to behave, the children of Israel had turned their desert settlement into a den of iniquity. When Moses returned from Mount Sinai, having the tablets with the word of God inscribed on them, he threw them down, breaking them at the base of a golden calf.

Contrary to what Mr. DeMille portrayed in his epic film *The Ten Commandments*, there is no scriptural account of the earth opening up and swallowing Edward G. Robinson or anyone else. In fact, a modern-day version of the film would more likely follow the account in Exodus, in which Moses, after looking out at the naked campers, instructs the sons of Levi to use their swords and kill all of the infidels (about 3,000 of them) in the encampment—because that was the

---

3. https://rsc.byu.edu/archived/sperry-symposium-classics-old-testament/law-moses-and-law-christ

commandment given to him by God, regarding the disobedience of those within His church.

The relevance of these incidents, the contents, as well as the context of the Old and New Testaments, has been lost through misinterpretation and time. In some cases, as in Psalms and portions of Isaiah, the works were written in a way to be memorized through oral tradition, which further confounded the masses.

As a twelve-year-old, according to some historical references,[4] the preteen Jesus was already teaching in the temple. For the skeptics, this otherwise unknown son of a carpenter would soon rise to become a controversial figure to whom both praise and condemnation were yoked—neither of which were asked for or deserved by the young man from Galilee, as all he wanted to do was the will of his Father:

> If ye had known me, ye should have known my Father also. . . . And he said unto them, Ye are from beneath; I am from above: ye are of this world; I am not of this world. . . . Then said Jesus unto them, When ye have lifted up the Son of man, then shall ye know that I am he, and that I do nothing of myself; but as my Father hath taught me, I speak these things. (1 John 1)

Adding to the frustration of the faith, the Roman empire wasn't the best place to practice this new-found Christianity or Judaism. After the mass slaughter of the general Christian population by Nero during the mid-70s, the disciples of Jesus went underground, forming house churches, with competing philosophies emerging almost immediately. New Testament accounts between Peter and Paul, for example, reveal differences in opinion about various doctrines, as well as how to govern the faithful followers of Christ, but both agree in the general form of who it was who stood at the head of the faith—the Lord Himself:

---

4. https://www.christianity.com/jesus/life-of-jesus/youth-and-baptism/why-did-jesus-go-to-the-temple-at-12-years-of-age.html

> Now therefore ye are no more strangers and foreigners, but fellow citizens with the saints, and of the household of God; And are built upon the foundation of the apostles and prophets, Jesus Christ himself being the chief corner stone. (Ephesians 2)

It's not every day that a man is born into the world, endures a lifetime of poverty (by his own choice), and then suffers torture and death—also by his own choice. Such was the purpose and mission of Jesus: to freely give up His own life, have the power to raise it back up and restore it, and thus redeem the human race.

Modern-day revelation and some Christian sects would argue that the most significant aspect of Jesus's life wasn't His death on the cross, but rather it was found in those few hours He spent praying in the Garden of Gethsemane[5] the night before He was taken to Golgotha.

With this shift in focus, away from the actual death of Jesus to the sanctified service He provided for all mankind (that being to pray for, suffer for and endure the pain of the fallen human race), the Atonement itself becomes the single most important event in the life of Christ. During His time in Gethsemane, Jesus—the literal son of God Himself—pleaded with His Father to consider removing the burden He was to endure there. In the end, however, even Jesus accepted the will of the one who sent Him as being adequate for the commission He accepted, and as a result, the pressure and strain of bearing the literal burden of all mankind was so intense that Jesus sweat drops of blood.[6]

Following His resurrection, and after a short return visit to the Holy Land, Jesus gathered His Apostles one final time and told them that He would be leaving for a while but that He would return at an appropriate time in the not-so-distant future. Now, almost 2,000 years since Jesus's departure, the Christian world still looks to the day of His promised return.

Scriptural references offer an early record of not only the "children of God" but also foreshadow and testify of the life and times of Jesus

---

5. http://anewregress.blogspot.com/2011/05/gethsemane-vsgolgotha-is-cross-really.html
6. https://www.christiancourier.com/articles/421-agony-of-gethsemane-the

Christ. The Bible has influenced the Christian world for hundreds of generations. As we examine its origins in the coming chapters, its many historical accounts may be noted to have spanned from the beginning of man, through the life of Christ, and into our future. Buried in the many biblical iterations and interpretations that the faithful followers of God have authored are important aspects that serve as spiritual pointers to what some Christian sects believe to be indications of a spiritual drought caused by the absence of God's kingdom on earth, which came at the death of the last living apostles around AD 100.

Some Christian faiths teach that the Second Coming of Christ opens the final chapter of the mortal probation of mankind. Jesus's return has been the subject of extensive debate almost since the moment He was carried into heaven after the Day of Pentecost. Although many cultures today and throughout history declared their insider knowledge as to when the Lord will return, the Bible notes that even Christ Himself does not know the day God will send Him back to close this final chapter.

So perhaps the question isn't, "When will he come back?" Rather, it is, "Will we be ready?"[7]

---

7. References:
   Isaiah Chapter 46
   Joel Chapter 2
   Daniel Chapter 12
   "Yahushua is the true name of the Messiah" (http://www.eliyah.com/nameson.htm)
   "Catholic Encyclopedia" (http://www.newadvent.org/cathen/08374x.htm)
   "A Comprehensive Etymological Dictionary of the Hebrew Language"
   "History of our Calendar" (http://www.webexhibits.org/calendars/year-history.html)
   "Calendar Origins" (http://www.calendar-origins.com/calendar-origins.html)

Chapter Twelve
To Turn Them from Darkness

"Rise, and stand upon thy feet: for I have appeared unto thee for this purpose, to make thee a minister and a witness both of these things which thou hast seen, and of those things in the which I will appear unto thee; Delivering thee from the people, and from the Gentiles, unto whom now I send thee, To open their eyes, and to turn them from darkness to light, and from the power of Satan unto God, that they may receive forgiveness of sins, and inheritance among them which are sanctified by faith that is in me."

—Acts 26

The word *vulgar* has a nasty connotation, but it wasn't always that way. There was a time when the term merely meant lacking good taste or being without education.

Most of the European blue-bloods of the early sixteenth century viewed any attempt at an English translation of the Latin Bible, also known as the Vulgate, as something akin to being unsuitable and downright blasphemous. In the 1500s, a common English translation of anything this side of Homer, Plato, or Socrates was considered less than favorable—especially the word of God.

And another word was borrowed to mean a range of nasty things in today's vernacular.

Some might find it ironic as well that the term's origins, "to make common" (which Jerome was attempting to do with his thirteenth century Latin translation of the Bible), appeared to be in opposition to the idea that God's word was for the general masses as well as for those actually conducting the Mass.

There's also the idea that God's teachings were meant only for those people (men) who were authorized to lead the church of the times, contrary to what was written in 1 Kings:

> Keep the charge of the Lord your God, to walk in His ways, to keep His statutes, His commandments, His ordinances, and His testimonies, according to what is written in the Law of Moses, that you may succeed in all that you do and wherever you turn, so that the Lord may carry out His promise which He spoke concerning me, saying, "If your sons are careful of their way, to walk before Me in truth with all their heart and with all their soul, you shall not lack a man on the throne of Israel. (1 Kings 2)

For more than a millennium, only Rome itself could dictate and interpret the words of Moses, Christ, and His Apostles, which had been locked away in Hebrew, Greek, and Latin translations and made available for public readings only by church leadership.

Many of the scholars of the day started asking questions, not only about the limited access to the scriptures but also of the real intent of the church in keeping commoners from gaining a better understanding of what was contained in what was considered to be "doctrine." How could God's faithful "keep His statutes" and "walk in His ways," as it was written, if they couldn't read, study, ponder, and fully comprehend what it was "He" was telling them to do?

You don't have to look any further than in the accounts of the religious bias of the day, and how protective the church leaders were of their sacred texts (or of the many frivolous taxes and fees they imposed on their faithful and often gullible congregations). And aside from early translations by Wycliffe and Erasmus—which both were seen as more experimental, than holy writ—the local leaders (religious as well as civil), didn't take too well to anybody, scholarly or otherwise, interpreting the Bible (and consequently, gaining a better understanding of its content) in the common tongue of the people.

Along comes young William Tyndale, a twenty-six-year-old second-year student at Oxford University who showed great passion for the common man (and maybe just a dash of hubris),[1] mixed with a generous dose of keeping with being one's "brother's keeper." As the Reformation marched forth in becoming part of the European fabric, its relevance became clearer through the original Greek translations from the New Testament. A young Tyndale made it his mission to ensure an accurate translation from Greek into English was unadulterated by the crown or the Holy See. A student of Erasmus, Tyndale was convinced that the word of God needed to be found as familiar with the farmer in the field as it was with the parish priest:

> I defy the Pope and all his laws. . . . If God spare my life ere many years, I will cause a boy that driveth the plow, shall know more of the Scripture than thou dost. (William Tyndale [1522])[2]

Religious curiosity, independent thought, higher learning, and mass communications converged in Europe in the early 1500s. Johannes Gutenberg's new development in bulk printing provided an affordable means of making the written word available in large quantities. Martin Luther's freshly translated German version of the Bible (along with his subsequent 95 points of concern against the Catholic Church)[3] became the period's version of a best seller and is considered by historians to be the tipping point for triggering the Reformation and launching the Protestant movement.

Tyndale, influenced by Luther, and a lifelong student of the Bible, took issue with the Vulgate translations as being too complex and

---

1. https://rsc.byu.edu/vol-17-no-2-2016/william-tyndale-john-foxe-boy-driveth-plough
2. https://www.christiantoday.com/article/william.tyndale.10.quotes.from.the.martyr.burned.for.translating.scripture/97290.htm
3. https://www.britannica.com/event/Ninety-five-Theses

took specific umbrage with the fact that most of the priests couldn't even read Latin.

He wrote about the word of God as being "the basis of salvation, and the grace of God its essence."[4] While his perspectives on the Roman belief of the "written word" was considered heresy by the Church (primarily because Tyndale challenged the dishonesty and arrogance of the priests), Tyndale's translation of the Greek and German scriptures into the common English tongue suggested his driving desire to reveal what he perceived as open corruption among the ranks of the clergy, as they controlled all aspects of religious education (and charged churchgoers for everything), as much as it was from his sense of public virtue:

> What a trade is that of the priests. They want money for everything: money for baptism, money for churchings, for weddings, for buryings, for images, brotherhoods, penances, soul-masses, bells, organs, chalices, copes, surplices, ewers, censors, and all manner of ornaments. Poor sheep! The parson shears, the vicar shaves, the parish priest polls, the friar scrapes, the indulgence seller pares ..... all that you want is a butcher to flay you and take away your skin He will not leave you long. Why are your prelates dressed in red? Because they are ready to shed the blood of whomsoever seeketh the word of God? Scourge of states, devastators of kingdoms, the priests take away not only Holy Scripture, but also prosperity and peace; but of their councils is no layman; reigning over all, they obey nobody; and making all concur to their own greatness, they conspire against every kingdom. (William Tyndale [1523])[5]

But the mid-sixteenth century, England wasn't comfortable with the idea that an upstart from Gloucester could possibly have the sense of the ages, to take the lead in translating the Bible for the common folk. As a result, Tyndale left Cambridge for more hospital conditions in Germany—the center of Lutheran thought—where, in 1525, he translated the Greek New Testament into English and forever linked

---

4. http://www.tyndale.org/tsj30/oliver.htm
5. https://m.egwwritings.org/en/book/1577.592

the messages of the Messiah with what he described as "the word of thy soul's health."

Tyndale, who spoke and wrote in the six "romantic" languages, was a master of English and spent the rest of his life in Germany and Belgium, translating and publishing his English version of the New Testament. In the company of close friends who leaned toward the new Lutheran way of looking at reforming the powerful hold the Catholic leaders had on their flocks, Tyndale, in his prologue of the 1525 translation, wrote:

> For who is so blind to ask why light should be shewed to them that walk in darkness, where they cannot but stumble, and where to stumble is the danger of eternal damnation.[6]

Center to that hold was the interpretation of God's word, and to his credit (as well as his ultimate peril), Tyndale's work on bringing the New Testament, and shortly afterward, his translation of the Pentateuch (with the assistance of Miles Coverdale), ultimately cost the forty-two-year-old scholar his life. Tyndale's efforts, however, resulted in 15,000 copies of scripture (in the "vulgar English") being distributed to rich and poor alike, and further inspired Coverdale to take up the cause "with the king's most gracious license" to produce what became the first authorized "standard works" in English.

Fast-forward 400 years. Just as Paul declared in Ephesians (and unlocked by Tyndale for the world to discover), Tyndale's passion as well as his peril laid the groundwork for what some would consider to be God's final chapter for mankind:

> In the dispensation of the fulness of times he might gather together in one all things in Christ, both which are in heaven, and which are on earth. (Ephesians 1)

---

6. Doctrinal Treatises and Introductions to Different Portions of the Holy Scriptures (Tyndale)

In Paul's first letter to the Christians at Corinth, he referenced the way in which God granted special gifts to people, in a way that would both, keep diversity and cooperation alive, while also advancing his word and his work:

> Now there are diversities of gifts, but the same Spirit. And there are differences of administrations, but the same Lord. And there are diversities of operations, but it is the same God which worketh all in all. But the manifestation of the Spirit is given to every man to profit withal. For to one is given by the Spirit the word of wisdom; to another the word of knowledge by the same Spirit; To another faith by the same Spirit; to another the gifts of healing by the same Spirit; To another the working of miracles; to another prophecy; to another discerning of spirits; to another divers kinds of tongues; to another the interpretation of tongues: But all these worketh that one and the selfsame Spirit, dividing to every man severally as he will. (1 Corinthians 12)

William Tyndale's work and Coverdale's subsequent complete manuscript of the Protestant Bible in English (with the Catholic Apocrypha as an appendix) gave way to what would become the "Great Bible," and ultimately, the foundation on which the Hampton Court Conference of 1604 would base their revisions to produce King James's "authorized version" (or KJV) in 1611. The Bible has become the most printed book in the history of mankind, fulfilling a commandment given by the Savior as written in the book of Mark:

> Go into all the world and preach the gospel to all creation. He who has believed and has been baptized shall be saved. (Mark 16)

Although executed in Antwerp in 1535, for the charge of "corrupting God's holy word," Tyndale's ultimate judgment by his peers has been left to the ages. He is commonly revered as "The Apostle of England"[7] and the forefather to the Bible in English for the world.

---

7. http://frcna.org/publications/item/8641-

Were it not for his work, as well as that of his student Coverdale's, which followed, King James might have been interpreted far differently. His dying wish was, "Lord, open the King of England's eyes!"

Tyndale died not knowing that Henry VIII had already sanctioned the printing of his version of the Bible for the masses, or that he contributed to the distribution of the most-read publication in human history.[8]

---

8. References:
   Isaiah 46
   Joel 2
   Daniel 12
   "Yahushua is the true name of the Messiah" (http://www.eliyah.com/nameson.htm)
   "Catholic Encyclopedia" (http://www.newadvent.org/cathen/08374x.htm)
   "A Comprehensive Etymological Dictionary of the Hebrew Language"
   "History of our Calendar" (http://www.webexhibits.org/calendars/year-history.html)
   "Calendar Origins" (http://www.calendar-origins.com/calendar-origins.html)
   1 Kings 2
   Mark 16
   Ephesians 1
   "Ninety-five Theses" (Encyclopaedia Britannica)
   Williams Tyndale's "Doctrinal Treatises ..."

Chapter Thirteen
Superior to Rational Creatures

"The God and Father, who holds the universe together, is superior to every being that exists, for he imparts to each one from his own existence that which each one is; the Son, being less than the Father, is superior to rational creatures alone (for he is second to the Father); the Holy Spirit is still less, and dwells within the saints alone."[1]

—Origen (AD ~215)

What becomes accepted as a common belief offers a certain level of comfort, which has historically lulled societies to form opinions and belief systems—often around word-of-mouth that has been handed down from one generation to the next. What was once defined as doctrine fades into legend and eventually becomes myth (like the idea that God could possibly be one of three distinct personages, as was accepted by the early faithful). By contrast, we're always discovering something new that, prior to that discovery, might have been considered fiction—or even heresy.

That's human nature.

1. https://iep.utm.edu/origen-of-alexandria/

What's also human nature is the desire to try to interpret and justify political dictates into dogma, such as the notion that the original creed should be interpreted as "God in three persons." Nowhere in the Nicene Creed does the discourse suggest God was three different people, and while modern Christian orthodoxy accepts such interpretations, much of those perspectives are rooted in ancient filibusters by princes, priests, and politicians.

Controversy surrounding the divergence between who God is and how He is depicted in the form of a "Holy Trinity" or "Godhead" gave rise during the first and second centuries. While Rome wrestled with the growing masses of Christian converts who continued to influence the way the empire worshipped its deity, free-thinkers were already shaping the ranks of believers on everything from which direction to point during prayers[2] to who was actually in charge in heaven.

Perhaps the notion of a divine threesome is partially due to the interpretations of the second-century Christian scholar, Origen of Alexandria, who posited:

> So that in this way the power of the Father is greater than that of the Son and of the Holy Spirit, and that of the Son is more than that of the Holy Spirit. (Origen [AD ~215])

Origen, the son of a martyred Christian philosopher, spent more than twenty years researching and writing about the books of the ancient scriptures, which—at the time—only consisted of the Old Testament. Origen evaluated the ancient writings based on three principles: literal writings, allegorical accounts, and moral messages. As no consensus of doctrine existed among the disparate congregations throughout the empire, Origen's early *De Principiis*[3] is often referred to as the foundation on which Christian philosophy is synthesized and blended into/with Greek and Roman ideologies. Origen's views on the Holy Trinity were based on a hierarchical model, with one divine being, "God in the fullest," sitting above all others, and the

---

2. https://www.enotes.com/homework-help/what-directions-which-christian-pray-god-354692
3. http://www.earlychurchtexts.com/public/origen_de_principiis_preface.htm

Son, "Logos Dunamis," and the accompanying Holy Spirit, being elected powers.[4]

Arius, another Christian leader from Alexandria during the latter half of the fourth century, argued that Christ was a divine being who was created by God (because of the consistent scriptural reference to him as the "Son of God"), prior to the formation of the world. Based on a sort of "celestial hierarchy" called "Neoplatonism,"[5] this concept of a sort-of divine trifecta has its origins loosely rooted in the writings of Justin Martyr, who was an early Christian apologist who died in 165. Justin, who was executed in Rome for not worshiping the gods, wrote: "No one with even the slightest intelligence would dare to assert that the Creator of all things left his super-celestial realms to make himself visible in a little spot on earth."[6]

Subsequently, any theological reference to a divine interaction between God and man, including the creation of the world, would not be undertaken—Justin supposed—by an Almighty Deity, but would have been undertaken by one who was assigned the responsibility and considered as the "Logos," or "Lord," or (as implied in earlier writings by Plato) as the premortal Jesus.

By contrast, Alexander, who was the current bishop of Rome,[7] disagreed, arguing that Arius's position implied Jesus as being less than God the Father, suggested some form of divine hierarchy (which further implied any Holy Roman Emperor may not be capable of divine rule).

Alexander believed Christ and God were of the same "essence," and soon, the controversy over the nature of God and His relationship to Jesus became central to religious debate throughout the empire. Add to the mix another perspective—one suggested by third-century priest and theologian—Sabellius.[8] In Sabellius' view, God was a single, indivisible entity, comprised of the Father, Son, and Holy Ghost.

---

4. https://plato.stanford.edu/entries/origen/
5. https://plato.stanford.edu/entries/trinity/trinity-history.html
6. Justin Martyr, *The Dialogue with Trypho* (London: SPCK, 1930).
7. http://www.newworldencyclopedia.org/entry/Pope_Alexander_I
8. https://www.newworldencyclopedia.org/entry/Sabellius

This form of "Monarchian modalism"[9] suggested a divine being in a God who could live, die, regenerate, and sanctify His comings and goings at will. And while seemingly outlandish by some standards (and a view that got Sabellius kicked out of the Catholic church by Pope Callistus in 220), with some sense of irony, some church scholars would suggest that in one interpretation or another, it is this divine modalism[10] that currently abounds as the core belief around God for today's current Christian population.

Such views, however, suggested a flaw in the rule of governance for ancient Rome and would not stand with the political factions (or the emperor).

At the beginning of the fourth century AD, Rome was replete with people claiming to have a portion of the original Church of Christ. There were many other interpretations of who and what Jesus was. In one case, a bishop from northern Africa actually believed that Jesus was sent to rescue mankind from a blind, crazed, fallen angel who had made the earth without authorization.

After his conquest and reunification of the Roman empire, Constantine turned his focus on matters concerning these disparate ideologies and also on deciding on what date the empire should celebrate Easter.

In the summer of 325, the emperor decided that at the expense of the government and under his personal supervision, all of the leaders of the various Christian sects would be gathered in Nicaea. Their purpose was to define, once and for all, the nature of Jesus and His role in deity. This council, he supposed (and declared), would quell the rising disputations among the faithful, regarding a notion that Christ was not divine but created in the flesh. Under the so-called "objective" guidance of Constantine himself, a vote was taken, and Arius's views were designated as heretical.

One fast track to breeding controversy is to second-guess the status quo, and that's what was happening in fourth-century Rome (and Arius was not only out-voted at the council, but he was also thrown out of the church).

---

9. http://www.newworldencyclopedia.org/entry/Monarchianism
10. https://www.theopedia.com/modalism

Out of that council of deep thinkers, philosophers, political figures, and pontificators came the Nicene Creed. The Creed, which established the foundation for Christian ideology, was an attempt to unify three centuries of interpretation about the nature of Jesus and His relationship to God and would define what has come to be referred to by the general Christian world as the "Holy Trinity" and establish more than 1,500 years of the fundamental Christian view on the nature of God and his relationship with Jesus.

Here's what the Creed actually says:

> We believe in one God, the Father Almighty, Maker of all things visible and invisible.
>
> And in one Lord Jesus Christ, the Son of God, begotten of the Father [the only-begotten; that is, of the essence of the Father, God of God,] Light of Light, very God of very God, begotten, not made, being of one substance with the Father;
>
> By whom all things were made;
>
> Who for us men, and for our salvation, came down and was incarnate and was made man;
>
> He suffered, and the third day he rose again, ascended into heaven;
>
> From thence he shall come to judge the quick and the dead.
>
> And in the Holy Ghost. (Nicene Creed [AD 325])[11]

Even though early Christian leaders conjectured on the nature and composition of the Holy Trinity, until Nicaea no one proclaimed the doctrine of the Trinity as currently accepted.

Almost sixty years after the Council at Nicaea, church leaders felt the need to revise the language further, while also financing the illumination and publishing of fifty volumes of authorized scripture, which would contain the first version of the "New Testament." These volumes were distributed to congregational leadership of "authorized" parishioners, with its content spread throughout the Holy Roman Empire, and provided the only allowed religious canon of the day, while also fostering conjecture over what God's word really meant to the common folk, and what God expected from His faithful followers.

---

11. https://www.usccb.org/beliefs-and-teachings/what-we-believe

By the beginning of the fourth century, the conquests of Constantine, who was also the first Roman emperor to convert to Christianity,[12] resulted in reunifying Rome under one leader. Perhaps out of hubris or in some twist of divine inspiration, the Roman regent decided to move the ancient capital of the empire from Rome to the ancient port town of Byzantium on the Black Sea. Historically recognized as the crossroads between Eastern Europe and everything else, moving the capital city to the newly named Constantinople planted the seeds of the destruction of the secular empire of the day, to be replaced by what became a religious empire throughout the world by the close of the first millennium.

Constantine's changing the central capital of the empire from Rome to what is now Istanbul had a significant impact on the religion of the day. It created a religious center in the eastern portion of the region, which was highly influenced by Greek tradition, while the city of Rome was left to the devices of local Christian leaders who claimed to be the official headquarters of the legacy Church of Christ.

Looking ahead 600 years, long after the battle between Leo and John[13] (the respective bishops of Rome and Constantinople in 588), to 1074, the Roman Catholic Church was fully established as the religious backbone throughout Europe and the known world. In an ironic twist of direction, religious domination was again in full swing in Eastern Europe and the Middle East, but this time, without any formal spiritual leadership sanctioned by God. Under the direction of Pope Gregory and the Roman Catholic Church, the first Crusades began, with a focus on ridding the Holy Land of the many religious "infidels" who inhabited it—namely, those who were not Christian (or Catholic).

By the beginning of the seventeenth century, the Roman Catholic Church was the governing body over virtually all of the Christian world.[14] The Vatican's position, strengthened through the Crusades,

---

12. http://www.thenagain.info/WebChron/EastEurope/ConstantineConverts.html
13. https://www.revolvy.com/main/index.php?s=Siege%20of%20Dorostolon&item_type=topic
14. https://www.museeprotestant.org/en/notice/the-catholic-reforming-movements-in-seventeenth-century-france/

would ensure a strong religious hold on political and religious heads of state throughout Europe. But a new era of enlightenment, which focused on secular independence and religious interpretation on the freedoms of worship, began to spread, largely as a result of Martin Luther's disenchantment with his Catholic leaders.

By the mid-1700s, a third generation of religious persecution was underway, as American colonists began to embrace new philosophies on prayer, baptism, and the role of religion in day-to-day life. The Church of England (having itself being formed after splitting from Catholicism) was not pleased with the influx of new religious ideas spawning in America, thanks mostly to the efforts of evangelists such as Jonathan Edwards and George Whitfield. For New England in the early 1800s, Christian ideology further fractured with the notion that a restoration of the pre-Nicene church structure has been reestablished in the form of a "latter-day restoration." With that "Great Awakening"—as was taking place in New England and across the Colonies throughout the period, the stage was set for the coming forth of a new religion, which did not descend from any of the existing Christian sects: Mormonism.[15]

The Bible states that God made each of us in His own image. With the advent of what is now referred to as The Church of Jesus Christ of Latter-day Saints ("LDS") and the revelations by Joseph Smith in the mid-nineteenth century, members of the LDS Church believe God is a glorified being who has attained eternal perfection in all things.[16] Though the thought of being compared to God would send many Christians into a stupor of fear and confusion (probably much like those fourth-century Christian scholars), Latter-day Saints believe that the ultimate gift God can bestow on His children is to give them all that He has. This, in turn, glorifies Him even more, just as earthly parents are edified by the growth, development, and success of our children.

Since God's ordained church vanished from the world, posits the LDS faithful, it would take the right combination of religious, political, and cultural conditions to allow the original church to be

---

15. https://www.mormonnewsroom.org/article/mormonism-101
16. https://newsroom.churchofjesuschrist.org/article/what-mormons-believe-about-jesus-christ

reestablished. There arose no better place than the colonial states of early America, or better time than in the early stages of a new nation, free from religious and political tyranny. The LDS philosophy holds that it was in the United States that God chose to restore His kingdom on the earth, as it was a chosen land, and the land on which he could reestablish a fulness of His gospel without it suffering another extinction.

As in the organized church during the time of Jesus, the restoration of fundamental church precepts would be comprised of a leadership of Twelve Apostles, who are called and ordained to the office by one who had received keys directly from the Savior Himself. The LDS faith sustains such a man as prophet, seer, and revelator, and believes en masse that he and the others within the Quorum of the Twelve Apostles were called, set apart, and ordained by direction of Jesus, through an unbroken line of authority that was restored to the Earth through the nineteenth century LDS church leader and Prophet Joseph Smith, which laid the groundwork to restore sacred truths and re-establish the Lord's Church in an inspired nation (America).

In a sense of modern alignment with the theologies of Origen and Arias, the rapid growth of the LDS belief system worldwide (now passing 16 million members)—which includes the idea that God is literally the spirit father of all mankind,[17] including Jesus Christ—was referenced by the ancient prophets on numerous occasions:

> And lo a voice from heaven, saying, this is my beloved Son, in whom I am well pleased. (Matthew 3:17)

> There came a voice out of the cloud, saying, this is my beloved Son: hear him. (Luke 9:35)

> "The Son can do nothing of himself, but what he seeth the Father do." (John 5:19)

---

17. https://www.lds.org/ensign/1989/01/prophecies-in-the-bible-about-joseph-smith?lang=eng

Whether out of curiosity or rooted in a deeper sense of divine purpose, humans seem to want to learn more about where we came from, why we are here, and where we will go when our respective lives come to a close. Motivated by such matters, a young boy in upstate New York did what now more than 16 million people believe to be a fulfillment of ancient foretelling:

> I had actually seen a light, and in the midst of that light I saw two personages, and they did in reality speak to me . . . and who am I that I can withstand God, or why does the world think to make me deny what I have actually seen? For I had seen a vision; I knew it, and I knew that God knew it, and I could not deny it. (Joseph Smith, Jr. [~1840])[18]

And like those fabled prophets of antiquity, the young visionary from New York would lead a following that has changed how Christianity may consider God and His eternal plan for the human race. Like those same prophets of old, young Joseph Smith believed so deeply in what he saw and held to be true, he gave up his life for it.[19]

---

18. https://www.churchofjesuschrist.org/study/manual/teachings-joseph-smith/chapter-1?lang=eng
19. https://www.churchofjesuschrist.org/study/manual/teachings-joseph-smith/chapter-46?lang=eng

CHAPTER FOURTEEN

THERE SHALL BE ONE MEASURE

"No free man shall be seized or imprisoned, or stripped of his rights or possessions, or outlawed or exiled, or deprived of his standing in any way, nor will we proceed with force against him, or send others to do so, except by the lawful judgment of his equals or by the law of the land. . . . To no one deny or delay right or justice."

—Magna Carta

The thirteenth century didn't start off so great for the new king of England. John Lackland, youngest son of Henry II and Eleanor of Aquitane, had inherited the largest empire in Europe in 1199. At the dawn of the thirteenth century, all of England, Wales, Ireland, and most of France was under one regent, thanks in part to his predecessor, Richard the Lion Heart.[1]

John, whose persona was depicted as the foil of the sixteenth century ballad "A Gest of Robyn Hode,"[2] was considered by history as someone less than favorable to sit on the throne. After the death of his brother, the not-so-lion-hearted sibling of Richard ascended to rule

1. https://www.britannica.com/biography/Richard-I-king-of-England
2. http://d.lib.rochester.edu/teams/text/gest-of-robyn-hode

England and began to conspire against everybody—including his two living brothers and their respective sons—especially Arthur (not that one)—who claimed the crown to be his. John allegedly oversaw the murder of his nephew, and legend proposes that this royal villain depicted in the legendary tales of Robin Hood and his so-called "Merry Men" was a treacherous monarch, a corrupt tyrant, a weak leader in war, and the most despised regent in the history of England.[3]

Within five years of taking the throne, John had squandered the wealth of a nation, lost vital land holdings to France, found himself in a civil dispute with English barons over rights of landowners, saw the territory of Normandy annexed by France, and was kicked out of the Catholic Church under Pope Innocent III. While some historians would look back and describe John's reign as ruthless, his initiatives to begin building what would become one of the most formidable navies in the world (as well as the famous London Bridge) stand as two major historical feats attributed to the wicked king.

John is best remembered, however, for signing a document that would forever define the way in which governments would consider the rights of those who were governed.

Following the catastrophic loss in a conflict between England and France, which plummeted Britain into near-poverty, and being left to sequester in Windsor Castle as a means of survival, John was surrounded on all sides by twenty-five prominent land owners (called "barons") who had seen enough self-pillaging of their respective country sides for the pleasure of the crown that they rebelled.

Under siege and financial stress, the incompetent king was forced by his land owners, subjects, and church leaders to concede to growing demands for equal rights regarding a range of matters, including the assignment of troops, tariffs, taxes, labor fees, and basic human rights of the common folk. On June 15, 1215, a reluctant king was pressured by the strong influence of the barons, who held the city of London hostage, and along the banks of the River Thames entered into an agreement that has influenced civil liberties and constitutional rights of the people for more than 800 years.

---

3. https://www.telegraph.co.uk/culture/11671441/King-John-the-most-evil-monarch-in-Britains-history.html

Based loosely on the ancient Anglo-Saxon law that was founded on the four basic freedoms—freedom of speech, freedom of worship, freedom from want or need, and freedom from oppression—the Magna Carta established the substance for incorporating these and other fundamental self-evident human rights into constitutions that have defined modern civilization (or at least tried to). While reluctant to sign and agree to the document, John was not a fan of the idea that God's laws would be above his own. The Magna Carta ("Great Charter") is held to be one of the most significant documents of human history and even became part of the formation of writings adopted by America's forefathers and influenced James Madison in his drafting of the Constitution of the United States[4] 500 years later. The document, which is only survived by four originals, established the foundation of rules that declare that everyone is subject to the law (including the king), as well as guaranteeing the rights of individual justice as well as the right to a fair trial by one's peers.

Life, liberty, and property were core tenets of human rights protected by the Magna Carta,[5] but its origins are deeply rooted in the relationship between man and a higher king, as its preface implies:

> Know that before God, for the health of our soul and those of our ancestors and heirs, to the honor of God, the exaltation of the holy church, and the better ordering of our kingdom. (Magna Carta)

Further examination of the Magna Carta has suggested that it was published at the behest of the church,[6] rather than just as a means of appeasing a potential civic disaster. Recent research conducted by Cambridge and King's College London has established further support that England had intended the Magna Carta to be distributed

---

4. https://www.loc.gov/exhibits/magna-carta-muse-and-mentor/magna-carta-and-the-us-constitution.html
5. https://billmuehlenberg.com/2015/06/16/magna-carta-the-christian-connection/
6. https://www.independent.co.uk/news/uk/home-news/magna-carta-new-research-sheds-light-on-the-churchs-role-in-publishing-world-famous-charter-10318826.html

throughout Europe because of the political infiltration of well-placed bishops as scribes who were charged with making copies for distribution, in an attempt to expand the church's locus of influence throughout Europe.

While the fact that the archbishop of Canterbury served as a liaison between the angry barons of England and their greedy king, historians further suggest that the document was also intended to serve as a contract between royalty and deity. The idea of keeping worldly kings under the continued scrutiny of heavenly hosts was nothing new by the thirteenth century. Some of the earliest scriptural writings regarding moral and civic justice and the relationship between God and kings abound in the Old Testament:

> Melchizedek king of Salem brought forth bread and wine: and he was the priest of the most high God. . . . He that justifieth the wicked, and he that condemneth the just, even they both are abomination to the Lord. . . . Judges and officers shalt thou make thee in all thy gates, which the Lord thy God giveth thee, throughout thy tribes: and they shall judge the people with just judgment. . . . Keep thee far from a false matter; and the innocent and righteous slay thou not: for I will not justify the wicked. (Genesis 14; Exodus 23; Deuteronomy 16; Proverbs 17; Isaiah)[60]

The assertion of the Magna Carta's stand on supreme rule was predicated upon the notion that a higher law (God's commandments) was uncontestable and must be followed. Beyond the laws of Moses, and further ratified by Christ, origins of the implied message of the Magna Carta also abound in New Testament dialogue, testimonies, and treatises, including the Gospel of Matthew, which foreshadow these fundamental principles of virtue in government and further establish that a king was not the law itself but subject to a higher law:

> There is therefore now no condemnation to them which are in Christ Jesus, who walk not after the flesh, but after the Spirit. For the law of the Spirit of life in Christ Jesus hath made me free from the law of sin and death. For what the law could not do, in that it was weak through the flesh, God sending his own Son in the

> likeness of sinful flesh, and for sin, condemned sin in the flesh: That the righteousness of the law might be fulfilled in us, who walk not after the flesh, but after the Spirit. (Romans 8)

Stephen Langton, the archbishop who served as moderator and coauthor of the original document, considered the righteous rule of not only the nation's current population but also its posterity, as he admonished his regent to consider the liberties of his subjects "inviable":

> John, by the grace of God, King of England . . . know ye, that we, in the presence of God and for the salvation of our soul and the souls of all our ancestors and heirs and unto the honour of God and the advancement of the Holy Church and amendment of our realm. . . . by this our present charter confirmed, for us and our heirs, forever; that the Church of England shall be free and have her whole rights and her liberties inviolable. (Magna Carta)

The rights and freedoms of England were granted by the Church as a result of interpreting the fundamental ideology of faith in Jesus Christ, and how New Testament laws and ordinances should be applied throughout English culture. Christian scholars have long claimed the Magna Carta as establishing a victory, not just for civil liberties but for the support of a divinely inspired government, which—as far as England at least—has stood for more a thousand years and which spawned the religious and civic liberties of the most independent and successful nations in the world: England, Canada, Australia, New Zealand, and the United States.

Now interpreted, intermingled, immortalized, deliberated, and debated by democratic governments around the world—and inspired by the words of a cadre of oppressed as well as righteous stewards—the Magna Carta established that the fundamental principles of life, liberty, and the pursuit of happiness must be observed by all, regardless of station, the origins of which being found deeply rooted in human nature to accept government rule based on the precept that the psalmist declared 2,500 years ago:

> The Lord Most High is to be feared, A great King over all the earth. . . . He rules by His might forever; His eyes keep watch on the nations. . . . Let the nations be glad and sing for joy; For You will judge the peoples with uprightness and guide the nations on the earth. . . . The Lord has established His throne in the heavens, And His sovereignty rules over all. (Psalms 47, 66, 67, 103)

A document that was written in 1215 can still sway nations and lead a people through tyranny.[7] That's what some scholars believe the value to be of the Magna Carta—more than 800 years after it was first written.

7. https://www.bl.uk/magna-carta/articles/why-magna-carta-still-matters-today

Chapter Fifteen
The Mere Pleasure of God

"There is nothing that keeps wicked men at any one moment out of hell, but the mere pleasure of God. By the mere pleasure of God, I mean his sovereign pleasure, his arbitrary will, restrained by no obligation, hindered by no manner of difficulty, any more than if nothing else but God's mere will had in the least degree, or in any respect whatsoever, any hand in the preservation of wicked men one moment."

—Jonathan Edwards (1741)[1]

The "Wonder of the world in this latter age for true happiness and felicity." Those are among the closing words of the opening text in the "authorized" version of the Holy Bible, wishing high regard for the son of Mary Queen of Scots, who took a bold first step in his new role as king.

As our journey continues through the pride cycle of history, a new era of understanding came out of the medieval period, which focused on secular individuality and religious inspiration on the freedoms of worship. This relatively puritanical perspective began to

1. https://www.ccel.org/ccel/edwards/sermons.sinners.html

spread, largely spawned out of Martin Luther's disappointment with his Catholic leaders, almost a century earlier.

Influenced by his dedication to the idea that salvation came through grace (rather than by good works), Martin Luther argued and opposed the further practice of granting indulgences, and as part of his newfound faith in God's grace, he authored the *Disputation on the Power and Efficacy of Indulgences* in 1517, which has been more commonly referred to as the 95 Theses. This list of rhetorical commentaries was posited as a means of initiating thought about how God, the church, its leaders, and the masses interacted, and how salvation was not a commodity that could be purchased and was just one of many issues James had regarding the somewhat jaded ways of the religious majority:

> Those who believe they can be certain of their salvation because they have letters of indulgence will in fact be eternally damned along with their teachers. . . . They who teach that contrition is not needed for those who intend to buy souls out of purgatory or to buy confessional privileges are preaching unchristian doctrine. . . . Any truly repentant Christian has a right to full remission of both the penalty and guilt, even without letters of indulgence. . . . Any true Christian, living or dead, participates in all the benefits of Christ and the Church. This is given to him by God, even without letters of indulgence. (Martin Luther [1517])

With the Reformation running at full speed across the European landscape, the Pope and his Catholic empire soon found themselves locked in a power struggle with an ambitious Protestant upstart from Scotland who would—much to the chagrin of Rome—stir up religious anxiety throughout the land as he would soon sit in St. Edward's Chair[2] in Westminster Abbey.

Mary's son, James VI of Scotland, ascended to the throne of England[3] in 1603 and forever unified the two nations as King James I of Great Britain. James had wanted to unite the religious

---

2. https://www.westminster-abbey.org/about-the-abbey/history/the-coronation-chair
3. https://www.britroyals.com/kings.asp?id=james1

factions—Catholic and Protestant—under one unified base of doctrine, under the auspices of the Church of England. Shadowing those efforts of the ancient Roman Emperor Constantine's councils some 1,300 years prior, the ruler of an empire again leveraged his political influence to establish a compromise between religious factions (with the added twist of everyone on both sides of the Catholic-Protestant debate would agree to certain political conditions).

Political and religious unrest in Europe, however, pushed the anxiety level from a stir to a boil eighty years before King James's move to unify the varied religious groups under one crown, when between 1604 and 1611, the Scottish king commissioned a group of scholars from throughout the British Empire to converge on Hampton Court and translate a new "authorized" version of the Holy Bible. This replaced what was commonly referred to as the Great Bible,[4] which had stood as the common tome of holy writ for hundreds of years. King James's authorized version displaced the Latin Vulgate as the standard works for English-speaking students of the word of God, garnering even greater rancor from Rome.

John Calvin, a sixteenth century Protestant[5] reformer and apologist, challenged the fundamental precepts of Christian doctrine and believed the idea that "scripture" was something akin to a spiritual education, inspired by God (whatever form it may be revealed):

> Scripture is the school of the Holy Spirit, in which, as nothing is omitted that is both necessary and useful to know, so nothing is taught but what is expedient to know. Therefore, we must guard against depriving believers of anything disclosed about predestination in Scripture, lest we seem either wickedly to defraud them of the blessing of their God or to accuse and scoff at the Holy Spirit for having published what it is in any way profitable to suppress. (John Calvin [1536])[6]

---

4. http://textusreceptusbibles.com/Great
5. http://www.christianitytoday.com/history/people/theologians/john-calvin.html
6. https://www.ccel.org/ccel/calvin/institutes.v.xxii.html

A pattern of enforced religious consistency and interpretation was about to resurface, which would consider how the faithful would interpret and follow the word of God, but with a twist: this boy-king of Scotland and England was a student of religious writings, in both Greek and Latin, as well as the works of John Calvin.[7] By the age of twelve, James was leading his government (with a few close advisers) and spurring on healthy debates regarding the puritanical nature of God at the Hampton Court Conference:[8]

> God has power to create, or destroy, make, or unmake at his pleasure, to give life, or send death, to judge all, and to be judged nor accountable to none: to raise low things, and to make high things low at his pleasure, and to God are both soul and body due. And the like power have Kings; they make and unmake their subjects: they have power of raising, and casting down: of life, and of death: judges over all their subjects, and in all causes, and yet accountable to none but God only. (King James I [1604])[9]

Various religious groups throughout Europe and the newly united British Empire were producing their own versions of what was to be called "scripture," along with individual charters for how to lead the faithful and pay the clergy. At Hampton Court,[10] James took charge and led discussions on matters concerning church government, prayer, and how to best translate the Bible.

The revised body of religious books that the young king had authorized followed Luther's lead and segregated what the Protestant king and his consorts considered to be uninspired, spurious books, written by various individuals, into an inter-testament section called "Books Called Apocrypha." These books, labeled "non-canonical" by Protestant leaders, were often included in the Protestant editions of

---

7. https://www.nms.ac.uk/explore-our-collections/stories/scottish-history-and-archaeology/james-vi-and-i/
8. https://www.britannica.com/event/Hampton-Court-Conference
9. James VI and I: A Speech to the Lords and Commons of the Parliament at White-Hall (1610)
10. http://www.historytoday.com/richard-cavendish/hampton-court-conference

the Bible of the times, but with the caveat, "These Books Are Not Held Equal to the Scriptures, but Are Useful and Good to Read."[11]

The Apocrypha[12] is composed of fourteen books that were originally part of the Greek Old Testament (although not part of the Hebrew-written Bible) but were considered canon by Hellenist Jews who lived in foreign lands during the time of Christ. The nine "accepted" Apocryphal books include:

1. **Ecclesiasticus**[13]—Written ~180 BC, this book includes proverbs and Hebrew life observations two centuries before the birth of Christ.
2. **Wisdom [of Solomon]**[14]—Many scholars hold up the Book of Wisdom as one of the most significant of the Apocryphal collection. Written about 65 BC, Wisdom was designed as a counterpoint to what many within the Jewish sects believed to be the excessive worldliness found within the Book of Ecclesiastes.
3. **1 Maccabees**[15]—Along with providing foundational literature for the Jewish festival of Hanukkah, this book by a Hebrew author living in Palestine was written 200 years before Christ and documents the death of Simon and the Maccabean uprising.
4. **2 Maccabees**[16]—This story also describes the Maccabean rebellion.
5. **Tobit**[17]—This popular book of fictional romance and philosophy was written around 300 BC and is purported to be based loosely on two prominent Egyptian stories that also incorporate one of the Jewish archangels, Raphael.

---

11. https://christianity.stackexchange.com/questions/7082/why-arent-the-biblical-apocrypha-included-in-the-protestant-bible
12. http://www.bible-researcher.com/canon2.html
13. http://www.sacred-texts.com/bib/apo/sir001.htm
14. http://wn.elib.com/Library/Religious/AP/Apocry_wisdm.html
15. https://www.biblegateway.com/passage/?search=1+Maccabees+1&version=NRSV
16. https://www.biblegateway.com/passage/?search=2+Maccabees+1&version=NRSV
17. https://www.britannica.com/topic/Tobit-biblical-literature

6. **Bel and the Dragon**[18]—This apocryphal book traces its history to the time of Daniel and the legend of the Babylonian dragon idol-god. Written a century before the birth of Christ, the Book of Tobit contains numerous references to future prophecies incorporating retribution.
7. **Judith**[19]—Strong female figures are seldom referenced as prominently in the scriptures as Esther, Deborah, Ruth, and Naomi, but the book of Judith centers around a widow of great influence who overcomes her enemies after killing the leader of the Assyrian army.
8. **[Additions to] Esther**[20]—Speaking of another great woman of scripture, authors from the first century BC returned to the Old Testament text and added clarification to passages in the original Book of Esther, which were ambiguous, but also to add depth and further impress upon the faithful, the magnitude of struggle between God and the adversary in the last days.
9. **Baruch**[21]—Named for and assumed written by Jeremiah's personal scribe, this book includes "The Epistle of Jeremiah."

While no longer considered canon by most non-Catholic Christians, there was a time when—before the Reformation—the sixteenth century Bible ("Geneva") considered the Apocryphal books to be read only as references:

> The books . . . which were not received by a common consent to be read and expounded publicly in the Church, neither yet served to prove any point of Christian religion save in so much as they had the consent of the other scriptures called canonical to confirm the same, or rather whereon they were grounded: but as books proceeding from godly men they were received to be read for the

---

18. https://www.biblegateway.com/passage/?search=Bel+and+the+Dragon&version=NRSV
19. https://www.biblicalarchaeology.org/daily/people-cultures-in-the-bible/people-in-the-bible/judith-a-remarkable-heroine/
20. https://jwa.org/encyclopedia/article/esther-apocrypha
21. http://www.jewishencyclopedia.com/articles/2565-baruch-book-of

> advancement and furtherance of the knowledge of history and for the instruction of godly manners: which books declare that at all times God had an especial care of His Church, and left them not utterly destitute of teachers and means to confirm them in the hope of the promised Messiah, and also witness that those calamities that God sent to his Church were according to his providence, who had both so threatened by his prophets, and so brought it to pass, for the destruction of their enemies and for the trial of his children. (Preface to the Apocrypha in the Geneva Bible)

Christian sects began to separate themselves and form around various interpretations of Christian principles pertaining to the Holy Trinity, salvation, and the relationship between life, liberty, and property. Amidst the growing expansion of ideas about what to believe, how to worship changed as well, from orderly congregational gatherings into emotionally charged revivals.

The spiritual awakening, which was fueled by this Protestant king and his fresh perspective on holy doctrine, further changed the way community thought. Philosophy, religion, and self-rule would evolve and give way to a journey by a group of pilgrim travelers to a place commonly referred to as the "New World."

Chapter Sixteen
Many Are Called

"Men's hands cannot be strong when God rises up. The strongest have no power to resist him, nor can any deliver out of his hands."

—Jonathan Edwards

"In the beginning." These three words foster all sorts of emotions, which may range from inspiration to anxiety, depending on our state of spiritual disposition.

From a unified concept among three of the most popular faiths on earth—Christianity, Judaism, and Islam—the idea that God created the universe and everything in it out of nothing in the beginning is a core precept. But the idea did not originate with the earliest writings of holy writ. The notion of something from nothing as part of the common thread among the three religions was a product of social evolution from the period following extensive political interpretations of the writings of the priestly authors of Genesis,[1] during the fourth century, and the political landscape of the time wasn't helping.

Given that historians and scholars have surmised that there are multiple sources of authorship comprising the final published version of the book of Genesis, the ancient writings that were ultimately

1. http://contradictionsinthebible.com/the-priestly-writers-reworking-of-the-yahwist-material-of-genesis-1-11/

collected and published as Christian scripture is replete with symbolism, myth, analogy (also known as "parables"), and gems of historical intersections.[2]

Scholars also reveal through patterns identified that the ancient tomes held as "sacred" can be loosely cataloged into four basic categories:

1. **Business affairs (epistles)**—The typical "epistle," as those found in the writings of the New Testament Apostle Paul to the various church branches throughout the empire, provided "official" directives for how the body of the Church should operate in consistency, regardless of location or political persuasion. These epistles became critical to further establishing the day to day operations in extending the Christian agenda throughout the Mediterranean regions and beyond.
2. **Chronological events**—These include accounts such as those in Exodus and Numbers and the books of the "Lesser Prophets."
3. **Witnesses**—Provided as firsthand testimonials by prophets and apostles (and a few women whose voices were counted as well), the key differentiator is that their accounts testify of the divinity of Jesus (or Jehovah). Such witnesses appear in Isaiah in the Old Testament, along with the songs and psalms of David and Solomon, and the traditional Gospels found in Matthew, Mark, Luke, and John in the New Testament. Other witnesses appear throughout the Bible.
4. **Commandments**—Reference to this category extends beyond the Ten Commandments included in Exodus 34 and include the many passages of legal guidelines included throughout the Old and New Testaments, including Leviticus and Deuteronomy, and the accounts of Jesus's teachings (especially His Beatitudes), as documented in the New Testament Gospels.

These four elements of divine writing provide the essential balance of direction, rebuke, and inspiration for man to live life under

2. https://web.cn.edu/kwheeler/Genesis_texts.html

the watchful eye of the Creator. Foreshadowing of things to come and prophesying of events are also essential to Christian thought, and the Bible includes numerous passages of scripture in which prophecies of events—some of which already having come to pass—including further revelation of thought, direction, and scripture.

As scholars examined the contents and context of the Old and New Testaments, much of what was written about how to behave in accordance with God's will (aka "Church life") has changed over time through different languages, cultures, and ideologies. In some cases, as in Psalms and portions of Isaiah, guidelines for how God wanted His followers to act, where He wanted them to go, and what He wanted them to do was clear:

> And this day shall be unto you for a memorial; and ye shall keep it a feast to the Lord throughout your generations; ye shall keep it a feast by an ordinance forever. . . . And in the first day there shall be an holy convocation, and in the seventh day there shall be an holy convocation to you; no manner of work shall be done in them, save that which every man must eat, that only may be done of you. (Exodus 12)

If scripture is to be judged on a historical timeline, God seemed to remain mum for almost 2,000 years, and the direction in which His worshippers were to take was lost to the ages. This became well demonstrated as the various Christian sects began to divide and appear[3] throughout the Roman Empire during the first five centuries after the death of Christ.

The impact of the Great Awakening resulted in unifying a central philosophy that became the fuel that flamed the passion of politics and religion in eighteenth-century America. Contrary to the status quo that supported the idea that the will of God was distributed by a regent or religious leader rang a hollow note to the rising number of individuals who discovered it was better to choose their respective paths for themselves. Removing the link between God and man, the

---

3. http://www.christianitytoday.com/history/issues/issue-9/church-at-home-house-church-movement.html

head-of-state was reduced to little more than a peer of the people, which gave way to the notion that man share in self-governing, but under the auspices of a Divine Creator.

The idea was that it would be an eternal king, rather than an early regent, who would inspire and establish those individuals to positions of authority, based on his eternal plan—in the spirit that "many are called but few are chosen." In the context of mid-seventeenth century England, being chosen to explore the New World meant a change of scenery and eventually a change of philosophy in every other aspect of life, liberty, and the pursuit of happiness.

Throughout the early sixteenth century, European explorers, including Spanish Jesuits, mapped the Chesapeake Bay. In 1583, England's "Virgin Queen" Elizabeth I approved Sir Walter Raleigh's quest to establish a plantation (meaning the creation of a community that would be "planted" in a foreign land) north of the Spanish territory known as Florida, although his attempts to establish the territory coined as "Virginia" in the queen's honor ultimately failed and subsequently cost him his head at the strong urgency of the Spanish government[4] in 1618 in retaliation for a violation of the 1604 Treaty with Spain by members of his expedition.

As the new king of Scotland, Ireland, and England, James I approved the first establishment, called "Jamestown" in his honor, by royal charter, in 1607, in the new Virginia Territory. The objective, according to the Virginia Charter, was to establish a ruling community of "certain knights, gentlemen, merchants, and other adventurers"[5] by the grace of God. But the founding principles of the law of the land may have its roots better connected to the writings of a handful of Pilgrim pioneers, rather than a Puritan prince.

Not only did he encourage and finance the monumental task of standardizing the word of God into what has now become known as the King James Version of the Bible, the Scottish king also undertook one of the most critically recognized experiments in the history of Western civilization: the independent colonization of a religious

---

4. http://www.history.org/foundation/journal/autumn01/jamesi.cfm
5. http://www.let.rug.nl/usa/documents/1600-1650/the-first-virginia-charter-1606.php

community, called "Virginia," on a continent more than 3,000 miles away from the ruling masses of the British Crown.

In some ways, James's vision of a utopian society on a distant land, where cultures, creeds, and colors could blend, backfired. Under his scrutiny, and later Charles I's oppressive rules regarding religious dissenters in Britain, hearts became stirred within a group of Puritans who chose to flee England. After their break with the Anglican Church, a group of English separatists turned their fealty to Amsterdam in hopes of starting new and independent lives. But Dutch life was difficult, and the work was hard for the English transplants. Concerned for their sense of identity as English folk among the Dutch, and possibly out of the growing tension between Holland and Spain, the settlers, led by Myles Standish and William Brewster, again boarded the now famous vessel known as the *Mayflower* and set sail west for open water, arriving in Plymouth Harbor in the New World after sixty-five days on the high seas of the Atlantic.

Seeking refuge and freedom from James's Church of England, forty-one religious separatists among the 102 passengers of the *Mayflower*[6] adopted the belief that since their ship had not landed at the English settlement of Virginia, but rather, in the unclaimed territory of Plymouth Harbor, their contract with the British crown and the Virginia Trading Company was void. Nonetheless, the settlers knew the risk and potential detriment of establishing a community without rule of law, and they entered into an agreement known as the Mayflower Compact:

> In the name of God, Amen. We whose names are underwritten, the loyal subjects of our dread Sovereign Lord King James, by the Grace of God of Great Britain, France, and Ireland King, Defender of the Faith, etc. Having undertaken for the Glory of God and advancement of the Christian Faith and Honour of our King and Country, a Voyage to plant the First Colony in the Northern Parts of Virginia, do by these presents solemnly and mutually in the presence of God and one of another, Covenant and Combine

---

6. http://www.plimoth.org/learn/just-kids/homework-help/mayflower-and-mayflower-compact

> ourselves together in a Civil Body Politic, for our better ordering and preservation and furtherance of the ends aforesaid; and by virtue hereof to enact, constitute and frame such just and equal Laws, Ordinances, Acts, Constitutions and Offices from time to time, as shall be thought most meet and convenient for the general good of the Colony, unto which we promise all due submission and obedience. In witness whereof we have hereunder subscribed our names at Cape Cod, the 11th of November, in the year of the reign of our Sovereign Lord King James, of England, France and Ireland the eighteenth, and of Scotland the fifty-fourth. Anno Domini 1620. (Mayflower Compact)

Navigating for what they had hoped to be the newly established colony of Virginia, and due to bad weather, the settlers landed in Massachusetts in Plymouth Harbor, setting in motion a chain of events that would transform an entire continent into a beacon of independent thought, religious freedom, and prosperity.

The Pilgrims recognized the need for the rule of law to govern effectively throughout a range of ideologies, if they were going to make their new colony survive—let alone prosper, while maintaining a close connection with the will of righteous governance. While the author of the Mayflower Compact is uncertain, likely candidates were the educated William Brewster and John Carver, who were among the forty-one men who signed and agreed to the charter for governing the new immigrants. Given their fealty to the Crown, the colonists agreed by virtue of the Compact that four core tenets would provide the guidelines for governance:

1. They would remain faithful to the British Crown.
2. They would live in accordance with Christian principles.
3. They would establish a single frame of community and agree to work together to build it.
4. The colonists would establish and abide by "laws, ordinances, acts, constitutions and offices" to benefit the fledgling colony.

Electing Carver as the governor over the Plymouth Colony in 1620, the group settled for the winter with only half of them surviving into 1621. By spring, their first governor and half the population of the Plymouth Colony had perished, leaving the rest to elect William Bradford to continue to govern based on what John Quincy Adams once referred to as "the original social compact," as the new governor and further establish the fundamental tenets of self-governance in the New World.

Scholars of colonial history often suggest that the rapid spread of ideology relating to self-governance (rather than slavery, taxation, or tossing tea into a harbor) was the impetus that ignited the American Revolution and the outward rebellion against another king of England. Unlike the distant past in the time of King John and the barons of Britain, however, the colonial farmers and landowners, religious leaders, and commoners no longer held their monarch accountable for the rising tide of tyranny across the land. They chose to do away with the monarchy altogether. Their assertion for religious, political, and economic independence[7] from any worldly crown was still very much rooted in their respective faith relating to the rule of law by a higher being:

> When in the Course of human events it becomes necessary for one people to dissolve the political bands which have connected them with another and to assume among the powers of the earth, the separate and equal station to which the Laws of Nature and of Nature's God entitle them, a decent respect to the opinions of mankind requires that they should declare the causes which impel them to the separation. We hold these truths to be self-evident, that all men are created equal, that they are endowed by their Creator with certain unalienable Rights, that among these are Life, Liberty and the pursuit of Happiness. (Thomas Jefferson)

Looking ahead a century later, past four major wars, countless skirmishes between settlers and natives, and a scorching case of smallpox later, the Colonies of America had become ripe for independence. Over the course of the seventeenth and first half of the eighteenth centuries, the colonies had developed into a lucrative source of commerce for England, as well as controversy, as the region known as "New

7. http://www.ushistory.org/declaration/document/

England" came under greater scrutiny by Britain, France, native populations who felt encroached upon, and the colonists themselves who had aspirations for expansion.

On the strength of such influences as those by Catholic evangelist Jonathan Edwards, who ministered to Massachusetts colonists in the mid-1700s (and who refused to be coerced into following his contemporaries into switching to Protestantism), a spiritual renewal ignited throughout New England, which evolved into what historians have referred to as the "Great Awakening."[8]

Some historians suggest Edwards's doctrinal and theological prowess were fueled by his capacity to successfully recap the main principles of Puritanism and the Reformation and apply those ideologies to colonial life's daily pursuits. Edwards believed as a fundamental belief of salvation that personal conversion was predicated on an open confession of one's faith and acceptance of Jesus as Lord and Savior. Without such confession, parishioners were not worthy (or allowed) to take the sacraments of communion. A student of John Calvin's teachings, Edwards was also concerned that God's children were spending too much time pursuing the things of the world, rather than be humbled and submissive before their Divine Maker:

> There is no want of power in God to cast wicked men into hell at any moment. . . . He is not only able to cast wicked men into hell, but he can most easily do it. Sometimes an earthly prince meets with a great deal of difficulty to subdue a rebel, who has found means to fortify himself, and has made himself strong by the numbers of his followers. (Jonathan Edwards [1741])[9]

In his 1741 sermon, "Sinners in the Hands of an Angry God,"[10] Edwards preached of a deity that was weary of the sins of men, and that "all wicked men's pains and contrivance which they use to escape

---

8. https://www.britannica.com/event/Great-Awakening
9. https://www.ccel.org/ccel/edwards/sermons.sinners.html
10. https://www.blueletterbible.org/comm/edwards_jonathan/sermons/sinners.cfm

hell, while they continue to reject Christ, and so remain wicked men, do not secure them from hell one moment."

One of the fundamental arguments associated with Edwards's outcry against material expansion was linked to the rising level of interest and exploitation of the colonists by their king across the ocean. Authoritarian rule, it seemed, lost its luster when separated by 3,000 miles of open sea. Further, given to mass assemblies by the general public, and far away from royal oversight, argument over independent thought replaced the common courtesies of the gentry as a means of discussing how to better understand the nature of God and His relationship with an independent soul.

Part Six
All Things Work Together

"This book of the law shall not depart out of thy mouth; but thou shalt meditate therein day and night, that thou mayest observe to do according to all that is written therein: for then thou shalt make thy way prosperous, and then thou shalt have good success."

—Joshua 1

Emmah. Tikvah. Zedakah. In the Jewish culture, the three principles of faith, hope, and charity[1] are central to the ancient "Maimonides 13 Principles of Faith,"[2] which are fundamental to every Jewish prayer book.

Included in the 13 Principles are declarations of faith that "all of the words of the Prophets are true," in a restitution and redemption for those who followed God (11), the coming of the Messiah (12), and ultimately, in a resurrection of the dead (13).

1. https://israelrevealed.com/wp-content/uploads/BMsummary48.pdf
2. http://web.oru.edu/current_students/class_pages/grtheo/mmankins/drbyhmpg_files/GBIB766RabbLit/Chapter9Maimonides13Princ/index.html

The three pillars of faith, hope, and charity were also central to Judaism's greatest Son—one who fulfilled Maimonides' twelfth and thirteenth Principles—the Resurrected Jesus Christ. Why, then, is there such a disconnect—almost willfully—between the Jewish faith and the followers of Christ, and will Judaism ever reconcile with Christianity?[3] Some Jewish scholars suggest that Jesus's Apostles, especially Peter, James, and John, never left their faith and remained tied to their Hebrew traditions throughout their lives.

Much of the furor over the prediction of a widespread conversion of the Jews to Christianity surrounds many of the biblical references made by Jesus and His apostles of a time when Israel would be redeemed. For the Christian faithful, the words, stories, and admonitions found in the Bible are guidelines for God's interactions and long-term plans for His people. Central to that plan was the state of Israel and its role in bringing to pass the immortality and eternal life of the human race:

> For thou art an holy people unto the Lord thy God: the Lord thy God hath chosen thee to be a special people unto himself, above all people that are upon the face of the earth. The Lord did not set his love upon you, nor choose you, because ye were more in number than any people; for ye were the fewest of all people: But because the Lord loved you, and because he would keep the oath which he had sworn unto your fathers, hath the Lord brought you out with a mighty hand, and redeemed you out of the house of bondmen, from the hand of Pharaoh king of Egypt. (Deuteronomy 11)

But even for His promised children, God had conditions relating to their achieving success in life:

> If ye hearken to these judgments, and keep, and do them, that the Lord thy God shall keep unto thee the covenant and the mercy which he sware unto thy fathers: And he will love thee, and bless thee, and multiply thee. (Deuteronomy 11)

---

3. https://www.quora.com/Is-it-possible-to-reconcile-Christianity-and-Judaism-so-they-are-both-true

Israel—and specifically Jerusalem—was most sacred to the Jews because of its ties to the patriarchs, Abraham, and David. To Christians, Jerusalem is center stage for the greatest story ever told and was the place where the Savior suffered (Gethsemane), died (Golgotha), and was resurrected (garden tomb).

What will be the final stroke of the pen on mortality? What will trigger those final closing moments, when, as was written by James almost two millennia ago, "the coming of the Lord is at hand[?]"

The belief in "dispensational premillennialism,"[4] which has its roots in the mid-nineteenth century Evangelical Movement, hinges on the nation of Israel experiencing a national awakening and subsequent turning to Jesus Christ as a sign of the last days before His imminent return. Ultimately, if such notions are to be believed, the Lord will return, restore Jerusalem, and reign in righteousness, as the Apostle Paul writes to the Christian faithful scattered among the Hebrews of Rome:

> Behold, the days come, saith the Lord, when I will make a new covenant with the house of Israel and with the house of Judah... For this is the covenant that I will make with the house of Israel after those days, saith the Lord; I will put my laws into their mind, and write them in their hearts: and I will be to them a God, and they shall be to me a people. . . . But Christ being come an high priest of good things to come, by a greater and more perfect tabernacle, not made with hands, that is to say, not of this building. . . . How much more shall the blood of Christ, who through the eternal Spirit offered himself without spot to God, purge your conscience from dead works to serve the living God? . . . So Christ was once offered to bear the sins of many; and unto them that look for him shall he appear the second time without sin unto salvation. (Hebrews 8–9)

By way of example, in the Gospel of Matthew, Jesus turns again to one of His favorite parable subjects, the ever-popular olive tree, for a reference to the natural versus grafted state of redemption (referencing the world of Gentiles who have been converted or grafted into God's

---

4. https://www.gotquestions.org/dispensational-premillennialism.html

favor), and a not-so subtle reference to God's "severity" for those who do not follow in their faith:

> Behold therefore the goodness and severity of God: on them which fell, severity; but toward thee, goodness, if thou continue in his goodness: otherwise,e thou also shalt be cut off. And they also, if they abide not still in unbelief, shall be grafted in: for God is able to graft them in again. For if thou wert cut out of the olive tree which is wild by nature, and wert grafted contrary to nature into a good olive tree: how much more shall these, which be the natural branches, be grafted into their own olive tree? For I would not, brethren, that ye should be ignorant of this mystery, lest ye should be wise in your own conceits; that blindness in part is happened to Israel, until the fulness of the Gentiles be come in. And so all Israel shall be saved. (Matthew 11)

Israel, in Jesus's parable, is again compared to a fig tree, whose growth sometimes fades and requires grafting of new branches to stimulate better growth and recovery. As the olive tree begins to blossom once again, he who owns the vineyard will soon come to tend to his garden.

For the Christian faithful throughout the generations of time, the conversion of the Jews has been a much-anticipated sign of the coming of the End of Days and a precursor to the Messianic Age.

Throughout history, Christian contempt for Judaism created levels of mass hysteria of historical proportions. From the Crusades, cries of "convert or die" became a common segregation point between the true believers and everyone else—especially the Jews. Following the establishment of the "blood purity" ordinance in Toledo, Spain, in the sixteenth century (part of the Catholic Inquisition), anyone of Jewish descent was rounded up and expelled from the country. Even those Jews who converted to Christianity were suspected of dubious intent.

Almost since the end of Christ's ministry and throughout the centuries that have followed, Christianity has anticipated the mass-conversion of the Jewish people to come to Jesus Christ as their Savior and promised Messiah. From Martin Luther to modern-day leaders, the Christian Church has considered conversion of the Jews as a preemptive sign of the return of Jesus. But when such a large-scale event will occur, at least according to one prominent Christian leader, is up to the Almighty and no one else:

> [The conversion of] Israel is in the hands of God, who will save it "as a whole" at the proper time. (Pope Benedict XVI)

Today, Israel is a thriving nation, restored to a stature it has never before experienced. Whether by state edict or cultural shift, Christianity stands by the core belief that Jesus is the Savior of the world, and that means He's the Savior to everybody—Gentile and Jew alike. When Christ does return to stand on the Mount of Olives, those chosen to be with Him will be those, the ancient prophet Zechariah writes, who will recognize His wounds:

> And one shall say unto him, what are these wounds in thine hands? Then he shall answer, Those with which I was wounded in the house of my friends. (Zechariah 13)

Chapter Seventeen
My Standard to the People

"Thus saith the Lord God, Behold, I will lift up mine hand to the Gentiles, and set up my standard to the people: and they shall bring thy sons in their arms, and thy daughters shall be carried upon their shoulders. And kings shall be thy nursing fathers, and their queens thy nursing mothers: they shall bow down to thee with their face toward the earth and lick up the dust of thy feet; and thou shalt know that I am the Lord: for they shall not be ashamed that wait for me."

—Isaiah 49

Ever hear of the term *Diaspora*?[1] After the Northern and Southern Kingdoms were finally conquered by the Assyrians and Babylonians, the people of Israel were dispersed throughout the various lands and kingdoms—either by force or by means of self-preservation and survival. This transformation of the children of Judah are called the Diaspora, referring to the Greek word that means to be dispersed.

1. https://www.lds.org/manual/old-testament-student-manual-kings-malachi/enrichment-j?lang=eng

Most of the bloodlines of Israel have been lost to assimilation into other cultures, which came because of their unwillingness to remain true and faithful to the commandments given to them by God through His prophets.

While the weak of spirit tend to blame God for their problems, history has shown that disobedience often results in consequences brought on by one's own actions:

> The Lord testified against Israel, and against Judah, by all the prophets, and by all the seers, saying, Turn ye from your evil ways, and keep my commandments and my statutes, according to all the law which I commanded your fathers, and which I sent to you by my servants the prophets. Notwithstanding they would not hear, but hardened their necks, like to the neck of their fathers, that did not believe in the Lord their God. . . . And ye shall be left few in number, whereas ye were as the stars of heaven for multitude; because thou wouldest not obey the voice of the Lord thy God. . . . And the Lord shall scatter thee among all people, from the one end of the earth even unto the other; and there thou shalt serve other gods, which neither thou nor thy fathers have known, even wood and stone. (2 Kings 17; Deuteronomy 28)

When the Assyrians captured the Northern Kingdom of Israel around 720 BC, after generations of warnings from Elijah, Elisha, and even Moses to repent and leave the ways of the world, idol worship, and following [2]false prophets, the fate of Israel began what would become thousands of years of conflict, captivity, displacement and Diaspora:[3]

> And among these nations shalt thou find no ease, neither shall the sole of thy foot have rest: but the Lord shall give thee there a trembling heart, and failing of eyes, and sorrow of mind: And thy

---

2. http://bibleresources.americanbible.org/resource/after-the-exile-gods-people-return-to-judea
3. https://dictionary.cambridge.org/dictionary/english/diaspora

> life shall hang in doubt before thee; and thou shalt fear day and night, and shalt have none assurance of thy life. (Deuteronomy 28)

Israel didn't just break the laws of their people; they violated their covenants with God by worshipping idols and even burning their own children as offerings! The people were ripe for conquest, which came swiftly to most of Israel by the hands of the Assyrians. Within fifty years of the capture of the Northern Kingdom, however, there was a new tide of power rising in the east. Nebuchadnezzar and his Babylonian empire moved swiftly against all enemies—including the mighty Assyrians and sweeping up what was left of the people of Israel in the Southern Kingdom of Judah.

But with most things relating to God and His children, the promise of redemption was offered, but only after great tribulation and persecution.

Following the assimilation of Israel, scripture offers little reference to what happened to the descendants of Jacob. Although Israel was no longer able to worship in a temple, the Babylonians did preserve a remnant of their heritage by allowing them to assemble and worship as they chose.

Whether out of their humility and return to their core values and faith, or because of some larger plan, the children of Israel were able to return (the first time in a series of comings and goings) to their promised land, following Cyrus of Persia's conquest of Babylon in 539 BC. Mentioned in biblical accounts more than twenty times, Cyrus the Great was considered by Jews and historians to be Israel's Great Liberator:[4]

> Who roused from the east him that victory hails at every step? Who presents him with nations, subdues kings to him? His sword makes dust of them and his bow scatters them like straw. He pursues them and advances unhindered, his feet scarcely touching the road. Who is the author of this deed if not he who calls the generations from the beginning? I, the Lord, who am the first and shall be with the

---

4. http://www.cais-soas.com/CAIS/History/hakhamaneshian/Cyrus-the-great/cyrus_the_great.htm

> last. . . . Thus says the Lord to his anointed, to Cyrus, whom he has taken by his right hand to subdue nations before him and strip the loins of kings, to force gateways before him that their gates be closed no more: I will go before you levelling the heights. I will shatter the bronze gateways, smash the iron bars. I will give you the hidden treasures, the secret hoards, that you may know that I am the Lord. (Isaiah 41, 25)

Although the return of the remnant of Israel to their former lands included a royal decree to build a temple to the Jewish God, in the spectrum of time, the occupation of Palestine by Israel's descendants was short-lived, following further persecution[5] and subsequent conquests of the region by the Egyptians, Romans, and in more modern times, rogue nations and foreign despots.

Through thousands of years of occupation, persecution, and the atrocities of the Holocaust, Israel has once again returned to its promised land, as prophesied by the sages. Whether out of the rising tide of European nationalism born out of two world wars or by caprice of political upheaval between the Ottoman Empire and Great Britain,[6] following a League of Nations mandate that gave Britain authority over the land called "Palestine," the Jewish homeland was reinstated and made sovereign and on May 14, 1948, David Ben Gurion.[7]

Although the nation of Israel now flies its sovereign flag above its capital city of Jerusalem, its people will continue to be a focal point in the struggle between God's children and the Gentile nations, a struggle of which Paul counsels in Hebrews:

> Cast not away therefore your confidence, which hath great recompence of reward. For ye have need of patience, that, after ye have done the will of God, ye might receive the promise. For yet a little while, and he that shall come will come, and will not tarry. (Hebrews 10)

---

5. https://www.adl.org/anti-semitism
6. https://owlcation.com/humanities/British-Foreign-Policy-Regarding-the-Ottoman-Empire-in-the-19th-and-twentieth-Centuries
7. http://www.jewishvirtuallibrary.org/david-ben-gurion

While in antiquity, the gospel and those who would acquiesce to its teachings were validated by their respective deeds. Religious leaders would deliberate on whether such "diversities of operations" and spiritual manifestations to advance wisdom and knowledge were not reserved for the period of the ancient prophets. Although Gutenberg never affixed his name to any book he published, his tribute by Pope Pius II in 1455 reflects on the man's legacy as being a man focused on quality in his work:

> All that has been written to me about that marvelous man seen at Frankfurt is true. I have not seen complete Bibles but only a number of quires of various books of the Bible. The script was very neat and legible, not at all difficult to follow—your grace would be able to read it without effort, and indeed without glasses. (Pius II, 1455)

But the mechanics of the press were only the instrument, albeit one of great impact on kick-starting the Reformation, Renaissance, and Enlightenment Era. Combined with the open expression of thought and interpretation in the written word, societies were primed for a cultural revolution. And that's just what happened.

Where friars and monks would have otherwise worked for days, sequestered in their scriptoria[8] to hand-publish one work—and then only in portions—the printing press with its moveable type was able to produce hundreds of manuscripts in their entirety, in a matter of hours. This allowed people more flexibility and access to knowledge across the range of topics and provided religious leaders to spread their versions of the gospel, and subsequently expand their locus of influence over larger congregations.

The Catholic Church almost immediately recognized the power of the written word and how it would influence and alter the mind, conscience, and motivations of society. Within forty years of Gutenberg's advancements in printing, Rome began requiring all books—religious as well as secular—to be screened and approved prior to being published. Although church censorship over publications had been

---

8. https://www.britannica.com/art/scriptorium

present for hundreds of years, once the ability to publish thousands of copies of a manuscript was out of church control, keeping central messages about faith, God, and fealty to the church would be akin to herding birds in a windstorm. Adding to Rome's anxiety was that the most sacred of all books—the Bible—was now being translated from Latin into various vulgar tongues of local dialects across Europe, which in turn also meant interpreting different perspectives of gospel stories, passages, psalms, and histories, based on syntax and word choice.

Printing in local dialects meant more people would have access to read something other than Latin—including women, who were in general never allowed to learn to read. Further, because of the advancement of mass printing, the way in which individual words were spelled became consistent, which provided a common context for even further translation of more texts. Ultimately, Latin became an archaic language, retreating to be found only in the halls of churches and universities.

By the time Columbus had reached the New World, Gutenberg's innovations in printing had spread throughout Europe. New written materials, including biblical passages, classical tomes (such as the *Illiad* and *Odessey*), historical treatises from Emperor Charlemagne, and the works by Chaucer and Dante were further influencing the masses. By 1500 more than 2,500 cities throughout Europe had acquired printing presses, and with the propagation of mass printing came the stimulation of curiosity, which led to deeper understanding of how things were managed (both in the church as well as throughout the various fiefdoms of Europe). Critical thinking, scholarship, and philosophy became consistent while also expanding to embrace more cultures and infuse more ideologies.

A Catholic priest with a penchant for asking questions will forever alter the philosophy of the faith of the masses.

Early sixteenth century religion in Europe had become something a notch above a convention of oligarchs. Abuse ran rampant throughout the cloisters as selling of certain ecclesiastical rites, absentee rule, and limited control over many by a few were all the rage in Rome. By 1517, many of the Catholic faithful demanded reform. Enter Martin Luther, a priest and professor of moral theology in Saxon-Germany, and his 95 Theses, which included arguments against the fee-based services now being rendered to the somewhat naive faithful—all for the purpose of funding the new St Peter's Basilica in Rome.

Thanks to the innovations brought forth by Gutenberg, Luther's 95 Theses were mass-produced and distributed from Germany to Rome (which garnered the attention of a disgruntled papacy and Pope Leo X, an often extravagant member of the de Medici family who was atop the Holy See). A debate that was initiated by Imperial order in 1518 saw Luther locking in a three-day argument with Cardinal Thomas Cajetan. The topic was indulgences and the defense of their use and support. Luther would have none of the Cardinal's claims and left the debate without resolution, given that the money was being funneled into a massive new construction, which now stands as the physical hub of the Catholic Church:

> Why doesn't the Pope build the basilica of St Peter's out of his own money? (Martin Luther)

Shortly after, the Pope issued a papal degree proclaiming Luther a heretic and his 95 Theses "scandalous and offensive to pious ears."[9]

The December 1517 printing of Luther's theses went viral, and as a result, the Protestant reformation was born, and further prophecy fulfilled, as referenced in Malachi:

> For from the rising of the sun even unto the going down of the same my name shall be great among the Gentiles; and in every place incense shall be offered unto my name, and a pure offering: for my name shall be great among the heathen, saith the Lord of hosts. (Malachi 1)

It would see that the Great Diaspora of Israel would now encroach into the powerful Christian faith based in Rome.

---

9. https://www.papalencyclicals.net/leo10/l10exdom.htm

Chapter Eighteen
Mountain of the Lord

"And it shall come to pass in the last days, that the mountain of the Lord'S house shall be established in the top of the mountains and shall be exalted above the hills; and all nations shall flow unto it. And many people shall go and say, Come ye, and let us go up to the mountain of the Lord, to the house of the God of Jacob; and he will teach us of his ways, and we will walk in his paths: for out of Zion shall go forth the law, and the word of the Lord from Jerusalem."

—Isaiah 2

As spiritual pilgrims across many faiths, we have been building sacred altars[1] to God for as long as we have been walking upright.[2] A surefire sign of the last days, according to Latter-day philosophy, is the need for and construction of not one but hundreds of temples to the Lord. In the days of Noah and Moses, God's dwelling place was always described as abiding in the mountains, such as the passages in the Old Testament in which God calls His children for

1. http://www.sacred-texts.com/bib/fbe/fbe028.htm
2. https://www.oldest.org/structures/temples/

further discussion, sanctuary, and redemption, from high and holy places, including Ararat, Horeb, Sinai, and Nebo:

> Now Moses kept the flock of Jethro his father in law, the priest of Midian: and he led the flock to the backside of the desert, and came to the mountain of God, even to Horeb. . . . And the Lord came down upon mount Sinai, on the top of the mount: and the Lord called Moses up to the top of the mount; and Moses went up. (Exodus 3, 19)

As referenced in the opening quote, the prophet Isaiah foresaw a time when the Lord would find a time in the spiritual evolution of humanity to once again establish holy houses—referred to by the Old Testament prophet as being "in the tops of mountains."

As far back as the book of Exodus, it is revealed that the children of Israel were instructed to "make me a sanctuary; that I may dwell among them."[3] This "House of the Lord," as it was referred to (and still is today), was a mobile edifice that was able to be transported with the children of God as they wandered from settlement to settlement. The tabernacle, its outer areas and adjoining anterooms, were all part of a process that was defined by God for the purpose of giving alms and dedicating His faithful, through blood offerings of firstlings of flock and field.

But Israel was not exclusive to the notion of temples being erected to God from a high position. From Babylon[4] to Rome, in Buddhist[5] and Hindu cultures,[6] throughout Asia and Africa—even in the United States, high ground has often been seen as a place equated with bringing man closer to his eternal maker:

> Even them will I bring to my holy mountain, and make them joyful in my house of prayer: their burnt offerings and their sacrifices shall

---

3. https://www.churchofjesuschrist.org/study/ensign/1972/01/ancient-temples-and-their-functions?lang=eng
4. https://www.britannica.com/technology/ziggurat
5. http://www.touropia.com/amazing-buddhist-monasteries/
6. https://en.wikibooks.org/wiki/Hinduism/Hindu_Temples

> be accepted upon mine altar; for mine house shall be called an house of prayer for all people. (Isaiah 56)

Once the children of Jacob (aka "Israel") had determined their homeland, they established a permanent house to give sacrifice to God. Often referred to as the "first temple" of Israel, it was created around 957 BC, during the period when Solomon, the son of David, ruled the kingdom. Designed in the symbolic shape of a man lying down, the first temple, also referred to as the "Temple of Solomon," was a place where the children of Israel could gather for sacrificial visits. Based on Old Testament and other Jewish accounts, the building was only about 30 feet wide and 90 feet long,[7] however, so things happened based on a schedule. The temple was also designated as the place where God would make His rule of law and literal presence manifest among His children:

> Thus saith the Lord, The heaven is my throne, and the earth is my footstool: where is the house that ye build unto me? and where is the place of my rest? For all those things hath mine hand made, and all those things have been, saith the Lord: but to this man will I look, even to him that is poor and of a contrite spirit, and trembleth at my word. (Isaiah 66)

This "first temple" included a couple of key fixtures, including:

- Storehouse (nearby)
- Courtyard
- Two Fonts
- Vestibule
- A Holy Place (for general worship)
- The Holiest of Holies (where the Ark of the Covenant would be placed)

---

7. https://www.sentinelsource.com/features/religion/cubits-sizing-up-noah-s-ark-the-temple/article_8468dfe1-2834-50be-a964-1edc817e3d35.html

Although different in purpose than the original temples to God—which were constructed to pay homage to the Eternal Provider of sustenance, crops, livestock, land, deliverance, and good health—modern-day temples are being constructed for the purpose of redeeming the eternal family of man, based on the LDS philosophy of redeeming our dead:[8]

> Else what shall they do which are baptized for the dead, if the dead rise not at all? why are they then baptized for the dead? . . . I say unto you, the hour is coming, and now is, when the dead shall hear the voice of the Son of God: and they that hear shall live. (1 Corinthians 15)

Essential to the redemption of mankind is the acceptance of the purchase Jesus made in the Garden of Gethsemane[9] for the atonement of each individual living in the past, present, and future, because they cannot see God or fulfill their own salvation without it. But what of those who never had the chance to hear of God's message, know of Christ or His purpose, or have the opportunity to participate in the covenants of salvation and the ritual washing (baptism) and redemption by the blood of the Lamb?

Although one predominant Christian culture—based in Salt Lake City—is often connected with its doctrine pertaining to the construction and use of holy temples,[10] the idea of performing vicarious baptisms for the dead, as well as other sacred ordinances, including that of eternal marriage, are considered essential tenets of an eternal sealing covenant between a husband, a wife and God, and have been echoed throughout various followers of God throughout the ages.[11]

---

8. https://www.churchofjesuschrist.org/study/manual/foundations-of-the-restoration-teacher-manual/lesson-16-redemption-of-the-dead?lang=eng
9. https://bible.org/seriespage/garden-gethsemane-luke-2239-46
10. https://www.mormon.org/beliefs/temples
11. http://www.jewishvirtuallibrary.org/the-first-temple-solomon-s-temple

While the Atonement of Jesus Christ[12] assures humanity that each of us will be resurrected and live in some state of eternal form, modern interpretation of scripture, including those passages found in Isaiah, Ezekiel, and Micah suggest that temple ordinances are part of the sealing power of God's eternal plan for his children:

> In the last days it shall come to pass, that the mountain of the house of the Lord shall be established in the top of the mountains, and it shall be exalted above the hills; and people shall flow unto it. And many nations shall come, and say, Come, and let us go up to the mountain of the Lord, and to the house of the God of Jacob; and he will teach us of his ways, and we will walk in his paths: for the law shall go forth of Zion, and the word of the Lord from Jerusalem. (Micah 4)

Modern-day interpretation of the sacred ordinances that were outlined in the early Church suggest that the time has been restored when temples should be constructed to perform vicarious ordinances for those souls who were not able to experience basic gospel tenets for themselves.

The idea of performing mediated work for those who have gone before us has its origins in the Atonement and sacrifice of Jesus Himself. When He atoned in Gethsemane and was nailed on the cross, Christian ideology holds that Jesus took upon Himself the sins of all mankind, past, present, and future. Thus, His sacrifice of redemption established the precedent for vicarious work.

As Isaiah, Amos, and others have prophesied of the House of the Lord being established in the mountains, God's people will retreat to those mountains to be further edified under covenant with Him in the last days. Prophets, both ancient and contemporary, foretell of a time in which the safest refuge from the rising storms of despair will be (with the exception of a faith-centered home) in God's holy temples, where God, upon the return of the resurrected Savior, will redeem His children:

12. https://bible.org/article/atonement-christ

> And in this mountain shall the Lord of hosts make unto all people a feast of fat things, a feats of wines on the lees, of fat things full of marrow, or wines on the lees well refined. . . . He will swallow up death in victory; and the Lord God will wipe away tears from off all faces; and the rebuke of his people shall he take away from off all the earth: for the Lord hath spoken it. . . . And it shall be said in that day, Lo, this is our God; we have waited for him, and he will save us: this is the Lord; we have waited for him, we will be glad and rejoice in his salvation. For in this mountain shall the hand of the Lord rest. (Isaiah 25)

Today, based on the philosophy of modern-day revelation as proclaimed by the LDS faithful, there are more than 265 temples either announced, under construction, or in operation in nearly sixty countries throughout the world.

Chapter Nineteen

Messenger of the Covenant

"Behold, I will send my messenger, and he shall prepare the way before me: and the Lord, whom ye seek, shall suddenly come to his temple, even the messenger of the covenant, whom ye delight in: behold, he shall come, saith the Lord of hosts. But who may abide the day of his coming? and who shall stand when he appeareth? for he is like a refiner's fire, and like fullers' soap: And he shall sit as a refiner and purifier of silver: and he shall purify the sons of Levi, and purge them as gold and silver, that they may offer unto the Lord an offering in righteousness."

—Malachi 3

The crowning accomplishment of his reign as King of Israel was Solomon's legacy of completing a temple to his God. In the ancient Hebrew capital city of Jerusalem, Solomon oversaw the construction and dedication of temple that would become the permanent holding for the sacred Ark of the Covenant, thus fulfilling what King David before him had been forbidden to do:

> Then David the king stood up upon his feet, and said, Hear me, my brethren, and my people: As for me, I had in mine heart to build an house of rest for the ark of the covenant of the Lord, and for the footstool of our God, and had made ready for the building: But God said unto me, Thou shalt not build an house for my name, because thou hast been a man of war, and hast shed blood. . . . And of all my sons, (for the Lord hath given me many sons,) he hath chosen Solomon my son to sit upon the throne of the kingdom of the Lord over Israel. (1 Chronicles 28)

Based on historical references, Solomon's temple included five altars that were located at various stopping points within the edifice and which were dedicated for specific types of offerings (whether for grain harvests, livestock, marriage civil affairs, and so on). The most sacred of all places—the Holiest of Holies—included two cherubim made of olive standing guard over the Ark of the Covenant. This sacred room was considered the place where God would dwell and was entered only by a high priest and only on one day of the year, designated as the Day of Atonement (Yom Kippur).[1]

Solomon dedicated lavish resources to the plan for his House of the Lord. The ancient Phoenician kingdom of Tyre to the north of Jerusalem provided the cedar for the timbers,[2] as well as quarried stone from surrounding mountains and mines, provided the edifice itself. In all, more than 3,000 teams and respective leaders were appointed to oversee the sacred task, as documented in 1 Kings:[3]

> Then Solomon assembled the elders of Israel, and all the heads of the tribes, the chief of the fathers of the children of Israel, unto king Solomon in Jerusalem, that they might bring up the ark of the covenant of the Lord out of the city of David, which is Zion. . . . And all the elders of Israel came, and the priests took up the ark. And they brought up the ark of the Lord, and the tabernacle of the

1. https://www.history.com/topics/holidays/yom-kippur-history
2. https://www.biblegateway.com/passage/?search=1+kings+5&version=KJV
3. https://www.biblegateway.com/passage/?search=1+kngs+8&version=KJV

> congregation, and all the holy vessels that were in the tabernacle, even those did the priests and the Levites bring up. (1 Kings 8)

This first temple,[4] which was destroyed in 586 BC, was a precursor to what has since become a standard for believers worldwide—both in the Christian faith as well as in others, in which the common belief is that God dwells in holy places.

The second temple, which was built by Israel following their liberation from Babylon, stood for 500 years but was destroyed by Rome in AD 70.

It was Malachi, however, who foresaw a time in which the Lord would return into His holy House and judge the world for their actions:

> And the Lord, whom ye seek, shall suddenly come to his temple . . . And I will come near to you to judgment; and I will be a swift witness against the sorcerers, and against the adulterers, and against false swearers, and against those that oppress the hireling in his wages, the widow, and the fatherless, and that turn aside the stranger from his right, and fear not me, saith the Lord of hosts. (Malachi 3)

That holy houses distributed throughout the world, including all related rites and activities, have all but faded from Christianity, with the exception of the Masonic rites[5] and the growing influence of The Church of Jesus Christ of Latter-day Saints as a Christian faith centered on Jesus Christ and His relationship with vicarious work for the dead. Jesus and the House of the Lord have been inextricably connected since He was a child:

> And the child grew, and waxed strong in spirit, filled with wisdom: and the grace of God was upon him. . . . And when he was twelve years old, they went up to Jerusalem after the custom of the feast. . . . as they returned, the child Jesus tarried behind in Jerusalem; and

---

4. http://www.jewishvirtuallibrary.org/the-first-temple-solomon-s-temple
5. http://www.freemason.com/how-to-join/what-is-freemasonry/

> Joseph and his mother knew not of it. . . . And it came to pass, that after three days they found him in the temple, sitting in the midst of the doctors, both hearing them, and asking them questions. . . . And all that heard him were astonished at his understanding and answers. (Luke 2)

On the day following Jesus's crucifixion, the Savior was, according to the Apostle Peter, in the spirit world teaching those legions of souls who had passed through mortality from the time of Noah onward:

> For Christ also hath once suffered for sins, the just for the unjust, that he might bring us to God, being put to death in the flesh, but quickened by the Spirit: By which also he went and preached unto the spirits in prison; Which sometime were disobedient, when once the longsuffering of God waited in the days of Noah, while the ark was a preparing, wherein few, that is, eight souls were saved by water. (1 Peter 3)

Like everything in the balance of God's eternal plan for His children, Jesus had a task while dead: to preach to those spirits that had not been afforded the chance to hear of his gospel, according to Peter's account:

> For this cause was the gospel preached also to them that are dead, that they might be judged according to men in the flesh, but live according to God in the spirit. . . . For the time is come that judgment must begin at the house of God: and if it first begin at us, what shall the end be of them that obey not the gospel of God?" (1 Peter 4)

The Bible is replete with references to a third temple,[6] but with those references come warnings of a time in which godlessness will follow the sacrifices made there, as in Paul's admonition to the Christian population at Thessalonica:

---

6. http://christinprophecy.org/articles/the-third-temple/

> Let no man deceive you by any means: for that day shall not come, except there come a falling away first, and that man of sin be revealed, the son of perdition; Who opposeth and exalteth himself above all that is called God, or that is worshipped; so that he as God sitteth in the temple of God, shewing himself that he is God. (2 Thessalonians 2)

This alleged man of lawlessness will, according to Paul, defile the temple by entering it and declaring himself as God. As far as the location of this third temple is concerned,[7] traditional Christianity suggests it will be reconstructed over the site of one of the previous two edifices, although modern-day prophecy suggests the new temple would be part of the adopted children of Israel, located in the New World. In his Revelation, however, John describes the triumph of the Savior's return over all lawlessness—especially that caused by the so-called Antichrist:

> For many deceivers are entered into the world, who confess not that Jesus Christ is come in the flesh. This is a deceiver and an antichrist. . . . Whosoever transgresseth, and abideth not in the doctrine of Christ, hath not God. He that abideth in the doctrine of Christ, he hath both the Father and the Son. . . . If there come any unto you, and bring not this doctrine, receive him not into your house. (2 John)

The reign of the Antichrist[8] as a religious and civic figurehead, according to prophecies in John's writings, as well as in Paul's writings to the Hebrews, will last for a period of less than four years, in which time he will go to Jerusalem and dwell within the rebuilt temple and act as God Himself. Those who oppose him will be persecuted, as his influence will sway religious, civic, and national leaders that he is God's true mouthpiece:

---

7. https://www.endtime.com/endtime-magazine-articles/time-build-third-temple/
8. https://www.biblestudytools.com/bible-study/topical-studies/the-rise-of-the-antichrist.html

> Little children, it is the last time: and as ye have heard that antichrist shall come, even now are there many antichrists; whereby we know that it is the last time. . . . Who is a liar but he that denieth that Jesus is the Christ? He is antichrist, that denieth the Father and the Son . . . and every spirit that confesseth not that Jesus Christ is come in the flesh is not of God: and this is that spirit of antichrist, whereof ye have heard that it should come; and even now already is it in the world. (1 John 2)

In addition to John, the Apostle Paul and the Savior Himself prophesied that defiling the third temple would occur as a sign of His return:

> When ye therefore shall see the abomination of desolation, spoken of by Daniel the prophet, stand in the holy place, (whoso readeth, let him understand). . . . Let no man deceive you by any means: for that day shall not come, except there come a falling away first, and that man of sin be revealed, the son of perdition; Who opposeth and exalteth himself above all that is called God, or that is worshipped; so that he as God sitteth in the temple of God, shewing himself that he is God. (2 Thessalonians 2; Matthew 24)

Regardless of whether it will be located in Jerusalem or some other city, the reconstruction of God's holy house is an inevitable sign of the times, according to ancient prophecy and modern revelation.

The Christian world, however, points to the time when the resurrected Lord—in the flesh—opens the doors of his temple(s), as a point in which God is validating His approval that Jesus is back, in charge, and quite literally taking names.

CHAPTER TWENTY

FAITH AND FELLOWSHIP

"My people hath been lost sheep: their shepherds have caused them to go astray, they have turned them away on the mountains: they have gone from mountain to hill, they have forgotten their resting place. . . . And I will bring Israel again to his habitation, and he shall feed on Carmel and Bashan, and his soul shall be satisfied upon mount Ephraim and Gilead."

—Jeremiah 50

What of the ten tribes?[1] The legend of the ten lost tribes of Israel has stood through generations of speculation. We know that Judah and his brother Benjamin established his eponymous kingdom in the south, through which today's remnant of Israel is said to have descended. But what of the other ten sons of Jacob?

According to ancient Jewish prophecy, one of God's revealed requirements for the world is that the original tribes of Israel will be reunited and all of their land restored. Historians and scholars from antiquity, as well as more recently, have evaluated, conjectured,

1. https://www.lds.org/bc/content/shared/content/images/gospel-library/manual/32506/32506_000_057_09-history.pdf

pondered, and pontificated on various verses and parsed passages of scripture in efforts to justify their respective understandings about the fate and anticipated return of these people. But who are these mysterious lost ten tribes,[2] and what happened to them?

The lost tribes of Israel have been debated and pondered for probably as long as they have been . . . well, lost. Following the covenant God made with the three patriarchs, Abraham, Isaac, and Jacob (whose name the Lord changed to Israel), Abraham's grandson sired twelve sons, who in turn each became head of their respective family lines or "tribes" (in order of birth):

1. Reuben
2. Simeon
3. Levi
4. Judah
5. Issachar
6. Zebulun
7. Dan
8. Naphtali
9. Gad
10. Asher
11. Joseph (later replaced by Ephraim and Manasseh)
12. Benjamin

Israel's faith in God was predicated upon what God had promised to do for them in the future, while God's covenant with Israel was based upon their obedience. The account documented in the book of Judges is based on the nature and general social decay of a new generation of Israelites who followed the children of Joshua. The new generation of Israel abandoned their religious principles and Talmudic teachings, and they traded their faith in God for stone and wooden idols of the surrounding influences, leaving them to face the world without knowing God:

---

2. https://israelinprophecy.wordpress.com/10-tribes/

> Moreover, that whole generation was gathered to their ancestors, and another generation grew up after them, who did not know the Lord or the work that he had done for Israel. (Judges 2)

As described in the book of Judges, the tribes were united by covenant with God but eventually shifted their religious and political focus to a more nationalistic form of rule. Because of the charismatic nature of the leaders of the time (this is loosely based on interpreted scripture), and especially due to the influences of civil unrest, the leadership hierarchy within the tribes eventually reverted to territorial rule. Traditions not sanctioned by the Talmud began to creep into the civic and religious philosophies of Israel as a people, including the worship of idols, which brought upon the children of God His unpleasant wrath and eviction from their promised lands:[3]

> The Lord shall cause thee to be smitten before thine enemies; thou shalt go out one way against them, and flee seven ways before them, and shalt be removed into all the kingdoms of the earth . . . the Lord shall bring a nation against thee from far, from the end of the earth, as swift as the eagle flieth; a nation whose tongue thou shalt not understand. (Deuteronomy 28)

As accounts from the Old Testament reveal, especially in the books of Leviticus[4] and Deuteronomy,[5] God's covenant people rejected His covenants with them and turned away from their obedience. Israel fell into a state of captivity and persecution, the undertones of which have resonated from the first century to the twenty-first. The greatest consequence for their disobedience, according to scripture, was the scattering of the original nation of Israel among more powerful nations, and the sacrifice of their lands:

---

3. See Judges chapter 2.
4. http://biblehub.com/leviticus/26-33.htm
5. https://www.biblegateway.com/passage/?search=Deuteronomy+8&version=KJV

> I will scatter among the nations and will draw out a sword after you, as your land becomes desolate, and your cities become waste. . . . The Lord will scatter you among the peoples, and you will be left few in number among the nations where the Lord drives you. . . . The Lord will scatter you among all peoples, from one end of the earth to the other end of the earth; and there you shall serve other gods, wood, and stone, which you or your fathers have not known. . . . I will scatter them among the nations, whom neither they nor their fathers have known; and I will send the sword after them until I have annihilated them. (Leviticus 26; Deuteronomy 4, 28)

After conquering a people, the Assyrians would relocate their captives far away from their native lands, forcing them to blend into Assyrian society and integrate with Assyrian bloodlines and customs. Eventually, the conquered cultures would become so diluted throughout the Assyrian empire[6] that they would cease to exist as anything but Assyrian.

Throughout the period when the kingdom of Israel was divided, scripture and other historical records note of a series of wicked rulers that took control of both the Northern and Southern Kingdoms. Chief among the problem was that Israel grew tired of listening to God through His prophets. They wanted a worldly leader—one who would bring them into their own glorious dominion.

God didn't agree:

> When they said, Give us a king to judge us. And Samuel prayed unto the Lord. And the Lord said unto Samuel, Hearken unto the voice of the people in all that they say unto thee: for they have not rejected thee, but they have rejected me, that I should not reign over them. According to all the works which they have done since the day that I brought them up out of Egypt even unto this day, wherewith they have forsaken me, and served other gods, so do they also unto thee. Now therefore hearken unto their voice: howbeit yet

---

6. https://www.historyonthenet.com/assyrian-empire-the-most-powerful-empire-in-the-world/

> protest solemnly unto them and shew them the manner of the king that shall reign over them. (1 Samuel 8)

Pekah was among the more wicked of Israel's petty rulers, and it was on his watch that God's prophecies began to come full circle. While the great patriarchs who had come before—Moses and Isaiah—foresaw a time of wickedness when God's children would fall out of favor, little did Pekah realize that his failure as a leader, and his desire for an alliance with the king of Syria, would plummet Israel into a struggle for legitimacy for almost 3,000 years. Around 740 BC, under the powerful leadership of Assyrian king Tiglathpeleser III[7] (aka "Pul" in 1 Chronicles), the Northern Kingdom was conquered and its people taken captive, while Shalmaneser[8] and Sargon[9] finished the job twenty years later, when they took the northern capital of Samaria. A century later, the Southern Kingdom of Judah (home of the people known as the "Jews") were conquered and dispersed by Nebuchadnezzar II and the nation of Babylon.

Although a remnant of Judah remained preserved, many of the Jews began to return to the land of Israel to settle and remained there until the Romans again destroyed Jerusalem in AD 70 and again in AD 135, which led to Israel again being scattered throughout the many nations of the world. While the descendants of Judah managed to retain remnants of their culture, history, and faith, the lost tribes remained scattered throughout the antiquities of time.

Although the children of Israel have been restored to a portion of their native lands, the literal gathering of Israel as foretold is considered by many Christian scholars as meaning far more than the lost tribes emerging from generational ambiguity.

But what may be lost to men is not lost to God.

Christian historians believe that one key prophecy relating to the return of the Savior—one that applies more to our future than our past—is that one of the important signs of the return of Christ will take place when the lost ten tribes of Israel are again reunited

---

7. https://www.ancient.eu/Tiglath_Pileser_III/
8. https://www.britannica.com/biography/Shalmaneser-V
9. http://www.ucl.ac.uk/sargon/essentials/kings/sargonii/

with their cousins from the tribes of Judah, Manasseh, and Ephraim. Some historians believe that Jacob's extended family—those descendants of the ten tribes of mention—were never really lost at all. Some Jewish scholars believe many of those individuals who were deported into Babylon (what is now the area of Iraq and Syria) never left the region but returned (eventually) to Israel in an effort to reclaim their homeland.[10]

Israel's many family branches may not be obscure at all—if we understand the history of God's people and how the world has grown up and around them. For the faithful, these people are not at all lost or hidden from God, and Isaiah knew that an "ensign to the nations" would be raised to signal the beginning of the return of all twelve tribes of Israel (including the two sons of Joshua: Ephraim and Manasseh):

> And he will lift up an ensign to the nations from far, and will hiss unto them from the end of the earth: and behold, they shall come with speed swiftly: . . . And in that day they shall roar against them like the roaring of the sea: and if one look unto the land, behold darkness and sorrow, and the light is darkened in the heavens thereof . . . And he shall set up an ensign for the nations, and shall assemble the outcasts of Israel, and gather together the dispersed of Judah from the four corners of the earth. (Isaiah 5, 11)

The revelation also includes blending Jewish doctrine with the restored truth of Christ, as He taught during His mortal ministry.

From Isaiah to John, the prophets foretell that in the last days, upon the triumphant return of the great Redeemer, "all the tribes of the children of Israel" will be united in faith and fellowship and will recognize Jesus as the one true redeemer of the world.

10. https://www.gotquestions.org/lost-tribes-Israel.html

Chapter Twenty-One
Kingdoms of Our Lord

"Why seek ye the living among the dead? He is not here, but is risen. . . . And it came to pass, that, while they communed together and reasoned, Jesus himself drew near, and went with them. But their eyes were holden that they should not know him. And he said unto them, What manner of communications are these that ye have one to another, as ye walk, and are sad?"

—Luke 24

The sky is definitely not falling (yet). As we wrap up our review of those various signs that may indicate our days as a mortal marathon are numbered, no study of Christian eschatology could be concluded without examining our perspective on how the human race is to be affected by the return of the Savior.

What happens when He shows up? Who's coming with Him? Who's going back? Who gets to stay (and why)? What will the earth be like during this period? And when is all of this going to happen?

There's a lot to unpack, as the modern cliché might suggest, regarding the days following the return of the Lord. There are a lot of armchair philosophers who believe they know the timeline and place of such matters.[1] Boiling down the material as it is presented in scripture, however, here's what many Christian faiths believe are the highlights:

Following the thousand-year period in which Jesus Himself presides over the world's religious affairs (the Millennium), there will be one last battle between Satan and the followers of Christ.[2] According to modern-day revelation, in this final, decisive, and epic confrontation, the good guys win, with Satan and his minions finally being cast out of man's presence forever (sounds like the makings of a great movie!).

With Satan out of the picture and the righteous followers of God (both living and dead) finding divine refuge, the world will be transformed into a glorified state, like it was when God walked with Adam and Eve.[3] Modern-day revelation proposes that all people who have ever lived on the earth will be resurrected and judged, and each individual will be granted an eternal reward, based on his or her obedience to God during mortality.

Not everybody lives at the same level of obedience, however, and as a consequence, upon the return of Christ, and as His divine restitution is being meted out, not everyone will receive the same rewards. The notion that "one size fits all" doesn't work when it comes to spiritual rewards and punishments, and contrary to a common belief that merely accepting Jesus as one's personal Savior is sufficient for eternal life, there's more to eternal life beyond "salvation."

True, the Atonement guarantees a resurrection for everyone, but what happens when we meet our Maker, according to New Testament authors—as well as Jesus Himself—depends on how we lived in mortality and goes beyond the atonement of our soul:

> Yea, a man may say, Thou hast faith, and I have works: shew me thy faith without thy works, and I will shew thee my faith by my works. . . . In my Father's house are many mansions: if it were not

---

1. https://www.ldsliving.com/5-millennium-myths-you-thought-were-true/s/76486
2. https://www.churchofjesuschrist.org/study/manual/new-testament-seminary-teacher-manual/introduction-to-the-revelation-of-st-john-the-divine/lesson-159-revelation-20?lang=eng
3. https://bibleanswers.study/will-the-nature-of-animals-change-in-the-millennium

> so, I would have told you. I go to prepare a place for you. And if I go and prepare a place for you, I will come again, and receive you unto myself; that where I am, there ye may be also. . . . There are also celestial bodies, and bodies terrestrial: but the glory of the celestial is one, and the glory of the terrestrial is another. There is one glory of the sun, and another glory of the moon, and another glory of the stars: for one star differeth from another star in glory. So also is the resurrection of the dead. (James 2; John 14; 1 Corinthians 15)

Three days after Christ was crucified, He was resurrected, reuniting a glorified body with His eternal spirit. Christianity teaches that until that time, no one had ever escaped the bonds of death. That event marked the beginning the first resurrection:[4]

> For the Lord himself will come down from heaven with a shout of command, with the voice of the archangel, and with the trumpet of God, and the dead in Christ will rise first. (1 Thessalonians 4)

When Christ was resurrected, many other righteous spirits came forth from the grave, according to ancient scripture:

> And the graves were opened; and many bodies of the saints which slept arose, and came out of the graves after his resurrection, and went into the holy city, and appeared unto many. (Matthew 27)

Based on the first resurrection of Christ, we are now living during this period, which started with Jesus Himself and will yet continue after His return, until all of the righteous souls are brought forth from the grave.

It is in this notion of a "restitution in all things" that the scriptures teach that all people who ever lived on the earth are entitled to the resurrection. However, the scriptures also note that not all people receive the same reward, and as such are not brought up at the same time. The first resurrection is the time when the most righteous of souls will be

---

4. https://www.gotquestions.org/resurrection-first-second.html

raised up to join Christ during His millennial reign on the earth and will join Christ to reign in an eternal state of glory.

The ancient prophets Isaiah, Jeremiah, Ezekiel, David, and almost all of the recorded Old and New Testament prophets wrote extensive passages with reference to the Lord delivering His people from the torments of the adversary, the demon, the dragon, the son of perdition, and other nefarious titles for Lucifer:

> The Lord shall send the rod of thy strength out of Zion: rule thou in the midst of thine enemies. . . . In the last days, that the mountain of the Lord'S house shall be established in the top of the mountains, and shall be exalted above the hills; and all nations shall flow unto it. . . . Behold, the days come, saith the Lord, that I will raise unto David a righteous Branch, and a King shall reign and prosper, and shall execute judgment and justice in the earth. . . . In that day, that the Lord shall punish the host of the high ones that are on high, and the kings of the earth upon the earth. And they shall be gathered together, as prisoners are gathered in the pit, and shall be shut up in the prison, and after many days shall they be visited. (Psalm 110; Jeremiah 23; Isaiah 2)

As part of this "restitution," the Bible tells us of numerous ways in which we can prepare ahead of time and how we can recognize the signs and events that will precede and follow the Lord's return. Among the many indications, here are four more commonly accepted events:

1. Jesus will reign as Supreme Leader.[5]
2. Satan will be bound.[6]
3. Death will be different.[7]
4. All truth will be brought forth.[8]

---

5. https://inspiration.org/christian-articles/the-millennial-reign-of-jesus-christ/
6. https://www.fbcch.org/files/1285/File/Revelation15.pdf
7. https://www.churchofjesuschrist.org/study/manual/gospel-principles/chapter-45-the-millennium?lang=eng
8. https://www.churchofjesuschrist.org/study/manual/doctrines-of-the-gospel-student-manual/37-millennium-and-glorification-of-the-earth?lang=eng

Jesus will reign as Supreme Leader

During His mortal ministry, Jesus made it clear that upon His return in glory, He would be the one in charge of all things. The following passage from Matthew reaffirms this conviction of the Savior's redemption of the human race (although probably not a good time for the "goats!"):

> When the Son of man shall come in his glory, and all the holy angels with him, then shall he sit upon the throne of his glory: And before him shall be gathered all nations: and he shall separate them one from another, as a shepherd divideth his sheep from the goats: And he shall set the sheep on his right hand, but the goats on the left. Then shall the King say unto them on his right hand, Come, ye blessed of my Father, inherit the kingdom prepared for you from the foundation of the world. (Matthew 25)

After judging the world, Jesus is foretold to oversee a thousand years of global peace:

> And I saw thrones, and they sat upon them, and judgment was given unto them: . . . and they lived and reigned with Christ a thousand years. (Revelation 20)

Satan will be bound

Just as God cannot abide in unclean places, Satan cannot stand in the holy presence of God. Chapter 20 in the book of Revelation is the only place in the Bible that mentions the period called the "Millennium." In this portion of John's "apocalypse," he refers to an angel "descending from heaven," which many biblical scholars infer to mean Jesus Himself:

> And I saw an angel come down from heaven, having the key of the bottomless pit and a great chain in his hand. And he laid hold on the dragon, that old serpent, which is the Devil, and Satan, and bound him a thousand years, And cast him into the bottomless pit, and shut him up, and set a seal upon him, that he should deceive

> the nations no more, till the thousand years should be fulfilled. (Revelation 20)

One of the most stark realities defined in divine law is that wickedness cannot stand in the presence of God, and in some ironic sense of contrast, wherever the embodied Christ appeared, it was always those wicked souls who first recognized Him:

> A man with an unclean spirit; . . . and he cried out, Let us alone; what have we to do with thee, thou Jesus of Nazareth? art thou come to destroy us? I know thee who thou art, the Holy One of God. And Jesus rebuked him, saying, Hold thy peace, and come out of him . . . And when the devil had thrown him in the midst, he came out of him, and hurt him not. (Mark 1; Luke 4)

As noted in the Gospel of Matthew, when unclean spirits were cast out, Jesus referenced it as a sign that the kingdom of God had come forth. Upon the Savior's triumphant return to reign on earth, Christian scholars have interpreted the prophets (old and new) to foresee Satan's illegitimate control and influence over the world being removed and transferring to the legitimate Lord, who—as Isaiah prophesied—will bear the "government upon his shoulders."

Death will be different

Again, in Revelation 20, John prophesies of a time when, upon the return of Jesus and the closing of the First Resurrection, the dead will not rise "until the thousand years were ended." Further, and often misunderstood, is the notion that death will not be present in the time of the millennial man. Not true. Isaiah references a time when children will grow to a ripe old age:

> No more shall there be in it an infant who lives but a few days, or an old man who does not fill out his days, for the young man shall die a hundred years old. . . . And they shall build houses, and inhabit them; and they shall plant vineyards, and eat the fruit of them. (Isaiah 65)

While death will surely come to pass on all of us, Isaiah's reference to children living out their lives to a full measure of their productivity and potential suggests that death will come only after a time when the men and women on the earth have had the opportunity to learn, work, live, and love—whatever that will be part of a quality of life while existing in a world where a resurrected Christ is in charge.

Some Christian scholars would also suggest that the absence of sadness and misery, as suggested in verses 18 and 25 of Isaiah 65, reference a time beyond the Millennium:

> Be ye glad and rejoice forever in that which I create: . . . The voice of weeping shall be no more heard in her, nor the voice of crying. . . . They shall not hurt nor destroy in all my holy mountain, saith the Lord. (Isaiah 65)

Interpretations of these passages might suggest that Isaiah is not looking just to millennial times and that his references to lions laying with lambs and an absence of pain and destruction suggest a time during Christ's eternal reign.

All truth will be brought forth

While we live in an age when information can be found on a myriad of topics, and in virtually everywhere the internet is allowed to be accessed, there is still much about the gospel plan that God has yet to reveal to the world. Moreover, there are still places in the world where Christianity is fragmented in its belief system. In his writings regarding the "restitution of all things," the Apostle John describes how the gospel will be spread across the land:

> And I saw another angel fly in the midst of heaven, having the everlasting gospel to preach unto them that dwell on the earth, and to every nation, and kindred, and tongue, and people, saying with a loud voice, Fear God, and give glory to him; for the hour of his judgment is come: and worship him that made heaven, and earth, and the sea, and the fountains of waters. (Revelation 14)

And finally, while the Christian populations throughout history have long awaited the return of Jesus, His imminent reign of peace and justice has been foretold for thousands of years—even before His mortal ministry. Just as when Jesus was born into the world, few people were aware of the significance of His birth, and the foretelling of His return has been interpreted by scholars, civic leaders, priests, and prophets.

While nobody (not even Jesus) knows the specific details relating to the return of the Lord, Christianity has got a pretty good idea of what to do to prepare for his return so that "ye also [be] ready: for in such an hour as ye think not the Son of man cometh" (Matthew 24:24). And one thing is for sure: If the world gets an extra thousand years to figure out which way to run in God's marathon, maybe a few more of us will make it across that sacred finish line.

Chapter Twenty-Two
Signs of Seven Thunders

"And I saw another mighty angel come down from heaven, clothed with a cloud: and a rainbow was upon his head, and his face was as it were the sun, and his feet as pillars of fire: And he had in his hand a little book open: and he set his right foot upon the sea, and his left foot on the earth, And cried with a loud voice, as when a lion roareth: and when he had cried, seven thunders uttered their voices. And when the seven thunders had uttered their voices, I was about to write: and I heard a voice from heaven saying unto me, Seal up those things which the seven thunders uttered, and write them not."

—Revelation 10

Being carried away in a vision of apocalyptic proportions is probably a scary thing. When John was so encumbered, he beheld an angel holding a scroll and who spoke with the roar of a lion. John writes that upon this angel's voice, "seven thunders uttered their voices," but he was forbidden to write down what was spoken. To Christians around the world, the penultimate purpose and objective of the life of Jesus Christ was found in His death upon the cross, as recorded in the New

Testament Gospels,[1] and His eventual return, coming in clouds of glory.

At the end of His brief visit back on earth after His resurrection, scripture documents that Jesus assembled His Apostles one final time.[2] He told them that He would leave them for a while, and—like so many parables of vineyards—that He would return at a designated time after the world had the chance to ripen a bit longer. Now, almost 2,000 years since Jesus's departure, when many would suggest that the "fruit" has fermented to a point of decay, the Christian world looks anxiously to the day when Jesus will return.

Christian theology supports the notion that the Second Coming of Christ will mark the closure of the final chapter of the mortal probation of mankind, and Jesus's return has been the subject of extensive discussion almost since He left. His return has been called the Great and Dreadful Day,[3] Rapture,[4] and End of Days.[5]

Although many cultures today and throughout history have claimed to know when the Lord will return, the scriptures record in the Gospel of Mark that even Christ Himself does not know the day God will send him back to us:

> Heaven and earth shall pass away: but my words shall not pass away. But of that day and that hour knoweth no man, no, not the angels which are in heaven, neither the Son, but the Father. Take ye heed, watch and pray: for ye know not when the time is. (Mark 13)

---

1. https://www.allaboutjesuschrist.org/prophecies-fulfilled-by-the-crucifixion-of-jesus-christ-faq.htm
2. https://answersingenesis.org/jesus-christ/resurrection/the-sequence-of-christs-post-resurrection-appearances/
3. https://www.lds.org/languages/eng/content/manual/old-testament-gospel-doctrine-teachers-manual/lesson-48
4. http://www.beliefnet.com/faiths/christianity/6-things-every-christian-should-know-about-the-rapture.aspx
5. http://channel.nationalgeographic.com/the-story-of-god-with-morgan-freeman/articles/the-different-meanings-of-end-of-days/

Everybody seems to have an insider track on the ultimate Christian events corresponding with the Second Coming of Christ. Philosophers, popes, prophets, and even a few politicians along the way have pondered on the return of Christ. Books have been written about it, songs have been sung, and plenty of wailing and gnashing of teeth has been done over false alarms throughout history. While many religious factions throughout history have their own take on the final disposition of mankind, of all three of the Abrahamic religions (Judaism, Christianity and Islam), Christians have our own unique, almost obsessive fascination with global mortality.

The advent of the Lord's return often begs one ultimate question—perhaps more of a curiosity—and that has to do with whether anybody can extrapolate an ETA for Jesus. While philosophers and scholars might want to debate the timeline of Christ returning from the heavens, even the Lord told us He would be the last to know when it was time to go.

And speaking of "seven thunders," here are seven key events that have been alluded as essential to occurring prior to His return:

1. The gospel will be preached to all nations[6]
2. Great tribulation, wars, and rumors of wars[7]
3. Drought and famine[8]
4. Disease and pestilence[9]
5. An opposing religious leader will rise[10]
6. Jerusalem will hang in the balance[11]
7. Signs in the heavens[12]

---

6. https://www.churchofjesuschrist.org/study/liahona/2010/09/the-gospel-shall-be-preached-to-all-the-world?lang=eng
7. https://www.northcoastcalvary.org/wp-content/uploads/2019/05/Jesus-in-the-Olivet-Discourse-.pdf
8. https://wol.jw.org/en/wol/d/r1/lp-e/101988244
9. http://www.christadelphianbooks.org/agora/art_less/p-q22.html
10. https://theconversation.com/five-things-to-know-about-the-antichrist-148172
11. https://www.jewishvoice.org/read/article/signs-times
12. https://www.beliefnet.com/faiths/christianity/6-heavenly-signs-of-the-end-times.aspx

The gospel will be preached to all nations

While Jesus sat at the Mount of Olives, His Apostles engaged Him on the matter of His ultimate return to them and what they should know regarding the world and his message:

> And many false prophets shall rise, and shall deceive many. And because iniquity shall abound, the love of many shall wax cold. . . . And this gospel of the kingdom shall be preached in all the world for a witness unto all nations; and then shall the end come. (Matthew 24)

Great tribulation, wars, and rumors of wars

The Gospel of Matthew includes Jesus's discussion with His disciples about the state of the world prior to His return as being "the abomination of desolation." The world has bathed itself in bloodshed since Cain rose up and slew his brother. The magnitude by which we kill each other, however, has risen exponentially, as was examined back in chapter 3, when we tallied the modern death toll of two world wars in excess of 100 million, not to mention the widespread coverage of the increase in mass shootings—even of children killing children! Jesus Himself shared this foreshadowing:

> Many shall come in my name, saying, I am Christ; and shall deceive many. And ye shall hear of wars and rumours of wars: see that ye be not troubled: for all these things must come to pass, but the end is not yet. For nation shall rise against nation, and kingdom against kingdom: and there shall be famines, and pestilences, and earthquakes, in divers places. All these are the beginning of sorrows. . . . Then shall be great tribulation, such as was not since the beginning of the world to this time, no, nor ever shall be. (Matthew 24)

Drought and famine

Two calamities that have historical context both in biblical times as well as modern day are the lack of moisture in the land, which usually results in a scarcity of food. Lack of water in the soil means plants dry up and crops die. Of all natural disasters, a "withering drought[13]" is only second in economic impact to a hurricane.[14] While the Bible is replete with stories of tribes waging war against each other as well as on the elements, modern history has experienced droughts so devastating—such as the Great Dust Bowl of the 1930s, the Northern Great Plains in the late 1980s, and Syria since 2007—that the land was permanently scarred, forcing whole communities to vanish. When crops die, so does livestock, and consequently we don't lag too far behind. It was true in the days of Moses as it is now, and Jesus warned us that prior to his return that there will be famines, as was just mentioned, but John also points to a future scarcity in supplies:

> And when he had opened the third seal, I heard the third beast say, Come and see. And I beheld, and lo a black horse; and he that sat on him had a pair of balances in his hand. And I heard a voice in the midst of the four beasts say, A measure of wheat for a penny, and three measures of barley for a penny; and see thou hurt not the oil and the wine. (Revelation 6)

Disease and pestilence

In war-ravaged places, there is often little left of conditions to sustain any kind of quality of life. Compounding such problems, in the absence of water and in the presence of mass starvation, other catastrophes often shadow the dead and dying. Jesus mentioned (and John reiterated) the increase in natural calamities in the world, like back-to-back-to-back category five hurricanes in the Gulf, massive landslides, perpetual winter "Nor'easters," and volcanoes and wildfires burning out of control. Flooding, fires, and droughts have always figured into God's rebuke of His children. Even the Old Testament books of Joel and Zechariah refer to earthquakes that have since been scientifically tracked to large-scale natural disasters from those respective periods. Moreover, both Matthew and Mark record that the Lord not only pointed to the sky from where He would someday return in glory, but He also looked to the earth itself for a sign of His impending arrival:

---

13. https://www.history.com/news/7-withering-droughts
14. https://list25.com/25-most-severe-droughts-ever-recorded/

> There shall be famines, and pestilences, and earthquakes, in divers places . . . For nation shall rise against nation, and kingdom against kingdom: and there shall be earthquakes in divers places, and there shall be famines and troubles: these are the beginnings of sorrows. (Matthew 24; Mark 13)

An opposing religious leader will rise

While Christianity remains the largest religious faction in the world and the largest of the three Abrahamic sects, it represents less than one-third of the global population,[15] with all other non-Christian faiths comprising the balance of the current population. In his three opening sermons found in the book of Deuteronomy, Moses admonishes the people of Israel to remain close to the word of God and not to become deceived by people (leaders) who would rise up among them and preach false principles that would appear to be truth. Centuries later, Peter counsels of similar false teachings:

> If there arise among you a prophet, or a dreamer of dreams, and giveth thee a sign or a wonder, And the sign or the wonder come to pass, whereof he spake unto thee, saying, Let us go after other gods, which thou hast not known, and let us serve them; Thou shalt not hearken unto the words of that prophet, or that dreamer of dreams: for the Lord your God proveth you, to know whether ye love the Lord your God with all your heart and with all your soul. Ye shall walk after the Lord your God, and fear him, and keep his commandments, and obey his voice, and ye shall serve him, and cleave unto him . . . But there were false prophets also among the people, even as there shall be false teachers among you, who privily shall bring in damnable heresies, even denying the Lord that bought them, and bring upon themselves swift destruction. And many shall follow their pernicious ways; by reason of whom the way of truth shall be evil spoken of. (Deuteronomy 13; 2 Peter 2)

---

15. https://en.wikipedia.org/wiki/Major_religious_groups

Jerusalem will hang in the balance

Almost since the beginning of its inception as a nation-state in 1948, Israel has been the center of Middle East controversy. While these social, cultural, and political burdens have been the bitter companion of Israel since Moses brought them out of Egypt, Jerusalem remains the epicenter of conflict and controversy, as it is considered a holy city by all three Abrahamic religions. But whether it be the Dome of the Rock or the Mount of Olives, the prophecies of old—from Moses, to Zechariah, to Luke, to Jesus Himself, the prophecies of Jerusalem being "surrounded by armies on all sides" may be closer to reality than just an idea:

> Behold, the day of the Lord cometh, and thy spoil shall be divided in the midst of thee. For I will gather all nations against Jerusalem to battle; and the city shall be taken, and the houses rifled, and the women ravished; and half of the city shall go forth into captivity, and the residue of the people shall not be cut off from the city. Then shall the Lord go forth, and fight against those nations, as when he fought in the day of battle. And his feet shall stand in that day upon the mount of Olives, which is before Jerusalem on the east, and the mount of Olives shall cleave in the midst thereof toward the east and toward the west, and there shall be a very great valley; and half of the mountain shall remove toward the north, and half of it toward the south. . . . And when ye shall see Jerusalem compassed with armies, then know that the desolation thereof is nigh. Then let them which are in Judaea flee to the mountains; and let them which are in the midst of it depart out; and let not them that are in the countries enter thereinto. For these be the days of vengeance, that all things which are written may be fulfilled . . . and Jerusalem shall be trodden down of the Gentiles, until the times of the Gentiles be fulfilled. (Zechariah 14; Luke 21)

Signs in the heavens

Through the closing decades of the twentieth century and into the current season, there have been numerous astronomical phenomena, including the return of Halley's Comet in 1986 and the additional comets, Hale-Bopp in 1995 and Hyakutake the following year. In the summer of 2017, North America and the United States saw the longest lasting total solar eclipse on record, and subsequent eclipses are due to appear in 2024, 2045, 2052, 2078, and 2099. In addition, the Aurora Borealis (Northern Lights), has increased in activity,[16] appearing as far south as the Caribbean. Although such phenomena have been attributed to increased solar activity and just good old-fashioned coincidence, Jesus and His prophets offer a different perspective:

> Immediately after the tribulation of those days shall the sun be darkened, and the moon shall not give her light, and the stars shall fall from heaven, and the powers of the heavens shall be shaken: And then shall appear the sign of the Son of man in heaven: and then shall all the tribes of the earth mourn, and they shall see the Son of man coming in the clouds of heaven with power and great glory. And he shall send his angels with a great sound of a trumpet, and they shall gather together his elect from the four winds, from one end of heaven to the other. . . . And the sun became black as sackcloth of hair, and the moon became as blood; And the stars of heaven fell unto the earth. (Matthew 24; Revelation 6)

In previous chapters, we looked at the events leading up to and including the time known as the Apocalypse and subsequent Millennium of calm that follows the so-called "great and dreadful day." And although even Jesus doesn't know the day of His return, for those who would study His words and recognize the signs of the times, His impending arrival should not come as a surprise.

Our objective: to recognize the signs and be ready!

---

16. https://www.forbes.com/sites/jillianscudder/2017/01/14/astroquizzical-aurora-solar-storm/#5e7e4be76bdf

Epilogue

Well heck, here we are—at the end of our little journey. If you have made it to this point, then I am grateful for your faith in spending time thinking this book could add value to your thoughts about the plan of salvation and what happens to us as we close our eyes one final time.

Regardless of our bias, I think it would be okay to say that a time will come when each of us will have the profound experience of standing at the judgment bar and reporting on how we used the gifts God gave us throughout our lives, in how we loved, how we learned, and how we shared those gifts with others. And like I mentioned in the opening chapters, there is no definitive tome on the subject of Christ's return and eventual reign on earth, but the scriptures are a pretty good place to remain when pondering such an eternally weighty matter.

As for me, it's off to the next writing project. But I am, again, grateful for your attention and faith in the time it took to get this far.

See you on the next journey!

Drew Blandford-Williams
December 7, 2021

Notes

Notes

Notes

About the Author

Drew Blandford-Williams was fascinated with stories from the Bible at an early age because of his grandmother, who read Bible stories to him. She died when Drew was nine years old, at which time he became even more interested in reading and learning about ancient civilizations and their relationship with God. More than forty-five years later, he has taught biblical studies for more than three decades.

Author of one of the multi-million-copy best-selling Complete Idiots Guides and hundreds of news articles over his forty-year career as a writer, Drew still enjoys discovering what he calls "unlocking the mysteries of the biblical authors" to learn how their writings foreshadow modern times. You can visit Drew at aboutdrewwilliams.com.

Scan to visit

aboutdrewwilliams.com

Notes